MERRY
THE BEST OF
BOTH WORLDS
IS HAVING A SISTER
WHO IS ALSO A FRIEND.
Pete
4-5-15

FBI
ANIMAL
HOUSE

FBI ANIMAL HOUSE

by

Peter M. Klismet, Jr.

HOUDINI™
PUBLISHING
www.houdinipublishing.com

PRAISE FOR FBI ANIMAL HOUSE

I enjoyed this book very much. The author nicely intertwined many of our crazy class experiences with the very real limitations, and outdated methods of our training. The only thing that saved most of the class was their own common sense when they were in the field.

Retired FBI Supervisory Special Agent
and member of this class

This book will keep J. Edgar Hoover spinning in his grave for years to come. Unless something has changed, most police academies provide a much higher quality of training than the FBI. What a shame! This book should be required reading for the bosses at the FBI. A very interesting and informative book that I highly recommend.

James M. Nelson, Assistant Chief of Police (retired)
Visalia, CA

I was a cop for 37 years, and am an FBI National Academy graduate. I found this book to be an accurate portrayal of what FBI training was like in the late 1980's when I was there. I thoroughly enjoyed the book and its true life, first person account of what FBI classes were then, and probably are now. The author has done a marvelous job with this book.

Sheriff James Black (Retired), Larimer County (CO) Sheriff's Department

I had absolutely no clue what I was doing after finishing the academy, and didn't begin to have one until I'd been an agent for about five years.

Special Agent Ed Mireles, FBI (Retired)

When I was with other federal agents, I envied their training as compared to mine. I was jealous. It was embarrassing to know we were probably the most poorly trained federal agency. *And we were the FBI.*

Retired FBI Special Agent and member of this class

ISBN: 978-1-936759-26-2

Library of Congress Control Number: 2014945064

Book Design by Blake Whiteside
Printing Production Specialist: Barry Hess
Edited by Robin Widmar

HOUDINI® PUBLISHING
www.houdinipublishing.com

Dedication

Thousands of FBI Special Agents have served honorably and performed near-miraculous tasks in spite of what I have characterized as very poor quality basic training. I want to express my sincere appreciation and admiration to them for what they accomplished, and what they did to keep this country safe. I believe what this displays is that the FBI did an excellent job in selecting agents who demonstrated intelligence, adaptability, and a high level of common sense. I salute you all for your work ethic and loyalty, and will always feel a debt of gratitude for what you have done for all of your fellow Americans. Which includes me. I am proud to have served my country as a Special Agent of the FBI.

I also want to extend my appreciation to all of the instructors at the FBI Academy, past and present. In no way is this book intended to impugn any of you or minimize your efforts to provide new agents with the best training you possibly could. The period described in this book, basically the 1980s and 90s, was a time of transition for the FBI. Newly appointed directors could not have been aware of the changes needed in training, in light of other demands of their jobs. The problem was a systemic one; the bureau had no interest in changing, and I hope and pray the needed changes have indeed been made for the training of new agents.

Our academy class has lost two highly regarded classmates, identified in this book under the pseudonyms of "Chip" and "Willie." Both of them were far too young when they passed away, and I believe the rest of my classmates share with me in mourning their loss. Both were great inspirations to all of us in their own and very different ways.

Finally, an FBI agent cannot survive the demands of his or her job without family support. I want to thank my two children and my former spouse, who regrettably died in 2013. You had to endure the months I was gone for New Agents training, and the many other occasions when I had to be away from home. I appreciate you all much more than you can ever imagine.

Acknowledgements

My wife Nancy has given me her complete support, enduring innumerable trips in a car holding a laptop while reading page after page, chapter after chapter to me, as we made changes to the original drafts of the manuscript. I have an amazing and patient wife, someone who puts up with my eccentricities, imperfections, and bad habits better than anyone could possibly deserve. I love you dearly.

I had an unbelievable editor for this book, Robin Widmar, who somehow managed to turn a chicken into chicken salad. She plucked out big and little errors, and noticed things you would never see by self-editing. Robin is incredible; I will never do another book without her, and if you need a high-quality editor for any of your written work, I couldn't recommend anyone higher.

My publisher's chief associate, Bernie Mateu-Consengco, has worked with me almost daily, and is chiefly responsible for this book being on bookshelves and the Internet marketplace and ready for readers. Bernie, it's been awesome working with you and the staff at Houdini, particularly Blake, who did the final design on the cover and back pages, and Barry, who sets up and prints off copy after copy. I also owe a debt of gratitude to Geno Munari, the president of Houdini Publishing, who immediately saw the potential in this book and quickly gave the go ahead to begin the publishing process.

Contents

Prologue		3
1.	The FBI's Involved: "We Give Up"	6
2.	The Job Is Yours if You Want It!	12
3.	Tell the Pilot to Land This Plane!	16
4.	Day One in D.C.	19
5.	Hoover's Grip on the FBI	23
6.	Swearing In as a Special Agent	29
7.	Day One at the FBI Academy	34
8.	Lunch and a Dose of Reality	37
9.	Origins of the Academy	42
10.	A Class on Bureau History	47
11.	Another Dose of Reality	53
12.	Firearms Training – Day One	61
13.	Special Agent Don Bishop	66
14.	And the Nicknames Begin	70
15.	Death by First Aid Training	77
16.	There Is a Doctor in the House	81
17.	Legal I	88
18.	First PT Test	92
19.	Stories in the Boardroom	96
20.	Jousting and Togas	104
21.	It's All About Marksmanship	110

22.	More Death—by Fingerprint Training	117
23.	Another Night in the Boardroom	122
24.	Worried about Legal II	126
25.	Passing the Tests Around	130
26.	The Controversial Miami Shootout	134
27.	The First FBI Academy	142
28.	One Wild Class Party	146
29.	Theft of Bird Guano Cases?	157
30.	The Boardroom: Home Sweet Home	162
31.	Willie the Golden Gloves Champ	171
32.	Preparing to Meet the Director	175
33.	A Brief History of FBI Directors	181
34.	FBIHQ Tour and Meeting the Director	187
35.	The Long Reign of J. Edgar Hoover	194
36.	White-Collar Crime and Photography	198
37.	A Night at the Officers Club	203
38.	Our Last Two Weeks	215
39.	Retrospective	223
40.	Graduation	230
41.	Why Stop the Party Now?	233
Epilogue		239
About the Author		244

Disclaimer

The views and opinions expressed in this work are those of the author, and do not represent the views and opinions of the FBI. The book was submitted to the FBI for pre-publication review and was approved.

This book is meant to portray the life and times of the people in it; however, some creative license has been taken to keep the flow of the story vital, clear, and intact.

Historical personages are mentioned by name. All other characters carry fictitious names. Some of the characters in this book represent a composite of more than one person or exaggerated traits, even gender, to emphasize a point. The same holds true for conversations, quotes and classroom lectures that take place throughout the book.

What is presented is not intended to be a transcript of conversations and other verbal discourse. Rather, it has been phrased in a manner intended to give the reader the general context of what was said.

Together, I hope the combination creates an informative excursion into a dimension of our world that very few people have ever seen.

Any errors are mine and mine alone.

Preliminary Comments

This book is based on my personal experiences while attending the FBI Academy in Quantico, Virginia. It is the first book to delve into the basic training of new FBI agents, as far as I know. It is a book which I hope will bring the reader to the frontier between myth and reality. Even with that said, few will believe it because the phrase "highly-trained federal agents" has been a part of our culture for many years.

While the book has already received positive comments from some former agents, it will not be universally popular with all current and former agents. I am well aware of that. But the truth is, there were very few changes in FBI Academy training (aside from a move to the facility in Quantico) between the 1930s and 1980s, or perhaps beyond. The characterization of "highly trained federal agents," while true in the 1930s and '40s, was anything but true fifty years later. The general public was led to believe the training of agents was the best possible. But here are some facts the public, politicians and even FBI Directors were not aware of: New Agents did not receive training in these areas:

1. **The steps involved in conducting an investigation.** (The standard catchphrase was "Check the Manual." But investigating a bank fraud case and a bank robbery in progress are completely different concepts.)
2. **How to conduct searches and collect evidence.** How to properly identify and handle evidence. How to take fingerprints. What types of technology were available to agents when they conducted their investigations.
3. **How to make an arrest.** What the procedure is if a person is arrested. What forms are to be completed?

4. **Use of Force.** We had no practical exercises and situational awareness of when the use of deadly force would be appropriate. There was absolutely no "Shoot/Don't Shoot" training aside from about five minutes on the "Hogan's Alley" course designed in the 1930s.
5. **How to write an FD 302, the basic FBI investigative report.** How to write a search warrant affidavit, an arrest warrant affidavit, or a wiretap affidavit. What the process is when returning a search warrant or wiretap evidence to the court.
6. **How to conduct a surveillance and/or talk on a bureau radio.** How to use pursuit driving skills (none were taught).
7. **Ethics** beyond the statement "Don't Embarrass the Bureau."
8. **How to conduct an interview,** let alone how to do an interrogation.
9. **Testifying in court.** We had a mini-lecture and brief demonstration in class one afternoon.

Regrettably, this is not an all-inclusive list. Unlike many police academies, few agents left the FBI academy prepared for their assignments in the field. Many said they were completely lost and had no clue what they were doing for several years, because they did not learn anything practical in their academy training. And, even worse, there was no formal training for agents when they left the academy. Most were simply on their own. Some never figured it out, served their time in mediocrity and retired. Had they received proper training for their job at some point, the FBI would have been a far more successful organization.

"The FBI is an entrenched bureaucracy that tends to be resistant to change..."

Former Supervisory Special Agent Gary Noesner
Stalling for Time, My Life as an FBI Hostage Negotiator

Prologue

Dan Blakely's last day in the FBI started out pretty much like every other day had in his first few months as an agent. He hit the snooze button twice, eventually rose, showered, dressed, and headed off to work. As he drove down the freeway, parked, and walked into the office, he had no clue that this would be the day he would kill someone.

Silhouetted against the pale glow of a dim streetlight at the end of a dark alley, Blakely could see the shadowy figure of a woman and the outline of what appeared to be a gun in her hand. That set off another type of alarm, one he couldn't hit the snooze button to stop. *Damn, it's a gun.* He was sure of it, and in those few brief moments, he knew he had to act.

It was Blakely's first stakeout since completing the FBI academy. He was excited when he was assigned to help some fellow agents on his squad locate and arrest a bank robbery suspect. Late that afternoon, a reliable informant had told the agents the man was holed up in a seedy hotel in the older downtown area. Blakely was sent to watch the back of the hotel.

But no one said anything about a woman accomplice, he thought. *She's definitely got a gun in her hand. Now what am I supposed to do? The academy trained us how to shoot, but they didn't tell us much about* when *to shoot*. Thoughts raced through his mind. He and the other FBI agents believed they had cornered a wanted man. Maybe the woman was the fugitive's girlfriend.

One of the best shots in his New Agents Class, but with no law enforcement experience before attending the FBI Academy, Blakely quickly raised and sighted his revolver. Three rapid shots found their mark and the woman fell. Blakely paused, his weapon pointed toward the lifeless form lying on the ground.

Hearing the unmistakable echo of gunshots, other agents involved in the fugitive search sprinted in the direction of the gunfire as the wanted man fled down the stairs and out the front of the building. But that was the least of their problems.

"She's hit!" an agent shrieked. "Jesus Christ, call a damn ambulance." His normally low voice was several octaves above its normal pitch. Again, he screamed, but this time into his portable radio. "Shots fired at this location! In the alley. Send an ambulance. Quick! We've got someone down." He radioed the location to a dispatcher in the FBI headquarters office, who quickly responded, "Confirming, you have shots fired and a person down. Ambulance is being dispatched to your location."

They leaned over the prone woman as a crimson pool spread onto the grimy pavement. An agent felt the woman's neck for a pulse. He didn't think he found one.

"Oh my god!" another agent screamed.

"What-what's wrong?" yet another shouted. "You okay?"

"It's-it's Donlan," the first agent stammered, looking over his shoulder as more agents arrived. "I think it's Sherry Donlan. Jesus Christ."

He glared at Blakely. "How in the hell could you shoot one of our own agents? We were just in a briefing together three hours ago."

Blakely stood there in a cold sweat, his body shaking, revolver at his side.

"Gimme that damn gun!" The agent frantically snatched the revolver out of Blakely's hand. "What the hell's the matter with you?"

Attracted by the gunfire and nearly hysterical shouts, two motley vagrants peered down the alley from behind a dumpster. "What happened?" one tattered man slurred, taking a huge gulp from his quart bottle of rotgut, MD 20/20 wine.

“Beats me,” his scraggly companion answered. “I think one of ‘em said they shot an FBI agent. I don’t wanna be a witness or something. Let’s get the hell outta here. Sounds like big trouble to me.” They slithered down the wall and silently crawled toward the opposite end of the alley, their prized bottle clinking lightly on the pavement, unnoticed by the agents hovering over the woman’s lifeless body.

The high-pitched wail of sirens sounded in the distance, echoing like a hungry pack of wolves in a mountain valley. The senior agent on the scene stared at the others, saying, “This can’t be happening. Tell me it isn’t happening. It’s gotta be a bad dream.”

But it wasn’t.

Reporters across the country droned on about “a highly trained FBI agent shooting another” in their morning newscasts. In the field, agents looked knowingly at one another, spoke in hushed tones, grieved and mourned individually. The loss of a fellow agent is a very personal issue, and each would deal with it in their own way.

Some understood, but others did not. Most knew that our training at the FBI Academy in Quantico, Virginia had prepared us quite well *how* to shoot a firearm. Many of us also knew that, among other things, we were barely trained in the most important part: *when* to shoot. In truth, the notion of a ‘highly trained FBI agent’ was simply myth and propaganda.

We wondered why it hadn’t happened before.

We wondered when it would happen again.

One

The FBI's Involved: "We Give Up"

Detective work can involve long, drudging hours of leg work, follow-up interviews, exasperating witnesses, and reluctant prosecutors. It requires the tenacity to stay with a case, even when it appears futile. And then sometimes you just get lucky.

Burglaries were plaguing homes and businesses in the east end of our pastoral, seaside town in Southern California. As a young, newly promoted detective, I was stymied. The crimes were occurring in the early morning hours, but the random array of days and locations made it difficult, if not impossible, to identify a regular pattern.

At the same time, my police chief was under considerable pressure from business owners, and was insisting to the Detective Commander that the string of burglaries come to an end. Not tomorrow.

Now.

I found myself working late hours and eschewing sleep, making the best effort I could to resolve the crime wave.

One late Friday afternoon I finally landed in the office, feverishly trying to catch up on paperwork, when I was summoned to the front desk. Typically, that meant a homeowner or business person was stopping by to see if any progress had been made on the theft from their place. Or perhaps to report some additional property missing. Or both.

This summons from the front desk would be the *exception.*

A week earlier, what appeared to be another in the continuing string of burglaries occurred at the local community college. The method of operation fit perfectly: early morning hours, door jamb pried or kicked in, etc. A classroom at the college was broken into and several items of electronic equipment were stolen, including two televisions and three video tape recorders.

A day after the burglary, one of the local FBI agents called the police department. "Hey P.J., it's Dave Irving, just checkin' in to see if you guys have got anything going we might need to know about."

"Not much," I replied. "We just had a burglary at the college that seems to fit in with the rest of 'em I told you about in the investigators meeting last week. Other than that, nothing I can think of."

"Well," Irving said, "why don't you let me check and see if that was part of a federal program? Wouldn't surprise me at the college. Lots of Department of Education funds go there. If so, we might be able to get involved and help you out a little bit. Never know. Sometimes two heads are better than one. I'll check and get back to you."

"Thanks, I'll catch up with you later." If the property was part of a federal grant, the FBI would take over as the lead agency on the case and I could close it out.

The next day, Irving called back. "Hey, guess what? The program they bought the TVs and video recorders from *was* federally funded, so you can refer it over to us if you want to."

"All right, will do. I'll send the reports over today. But we'll stay in touch, right? I want to make sure we get the guys if possible." The FBI was somewhat known to take a lot of information, but not to give a whole lot back in return.

"No problem. I'll keep you apprised of whatever I find out. Same with you, right?"

"Oh, yeah. You can count on that."

Now if someone from the college called, I could tell them, “The FBI’s working the case.” They’d be impressed, even though the case would probably never be solved.

I hung up and went into my lieutenant’s office, announcing, “Hey boss, we can write one off the books. The FBI just took the case at the college. It looks like the property was part of a federal grant. So they’ve got it. I’ll stay in touch, though.”

“Good thinking.” He stacked up some papers and looked up. “What do you think about writing up a little press release for the paper tomorrow? You might say something about the case, what they took, and that we’re working with the FBI. You can figure the rest out. Maybe a little publicity will produce a witness or some new information. Can’t hurt. You got time to write something up?”

“Sure, no problem.”

The following day, a short article appeared on the back page of the local newspaper. “FBI Investigating Theft at College” was the headline. The short accompanying story told readers about the stolen property having been purchased with money from a federally funded government program. “Because of this,” the article said, “the FBI has assumed jurisdiction and will head up the investigation.”

As if it was a *big* investigation. The amount of property stolen barely cost the school a thousand dollars, which paled in comparison to some of the other burglaries we had in the preceding months.

Shortly after lunch the phone on my desk rang and I was summoned to the reception area in the front of the police station.

“Detective,” the desk sergeant said, pointing at two young men standing beside the desk. “These two guys want to turn themselves in.”

I looked at the sergeant and then at the two men. "For what?"

"That burglary at the college last week."

"You're kidding me."

"Nope. That's what they said. I'll let *you* get the rest of the story out of them. That's all they told me, and since I don't know all the facts of the case, I figured I'd better get you to talk with 'em."

Nodding toward the sergeant, I took a look at the two young men. "So, are you saying you're the guys who did the burglary?" I asked.

"Yup," one of them answered. He looked down at his feet, then back up at the sergeant, avoiding my stare. He was a bit of a scraggly looking young man, about nineteen years old, and his partner didn't look like he shopped at a high quality men's store for his haberdashery either.

"Well, okay then, why don't you guys follow me? Let's go back and talk about this for a while." I looked at the desk sergeant, shrugged, and raised my hands, palms upward.

We headed down the hallway and into the Detective Bureau. I split them up in separate interview rooms, and by the time I finished interviewing them, their stories were virtually the same. Both readily owned up to the burglary at the college, and copped out to nearly all of the others I'd been investigating. But I found the most startling part of the interview to be the answer to the question, "Why did you decide to turn yourselves in?"

"Because we heard the FBI was investigating the case." Both answered it the same way. While neither young man appeared to be candidates for the dean's list, I was astonished by the answer. "We talked it over after we saw the paper," the brighter appearing of the two said. "When we heard the FBI was handling the investigation, we figured we might as well just give up. No point in messing with those guys."

"So let me see if I've got this right. You figured you might as well turn yourself in, since the FBI was eventually going to catch up with you? There's no other reason?" I still have no clue how I kept a straight face when I asked this question.

"That's right."

One of the young men offered up another valuable nugget of his thought process. "My social studies teacher told us the FBI was tapping everyone's phones and they were investigating everybody in the country. So I figured they'd get us eventually."

At that point all I could do was laugh out loud. I'm still not sure if he understood why.

The next day, I called my counterpart at the local FBI office. "Hey Dave. I just want to let you know we got the guys who did the burglary at the college."

He sounded very excited. "No kidding. That's great! What happened?"

I started out laughing. "Well, you might not believe this, but here's the story. These two nitwits came in yesterday and said they heard the FBI was on the case, so they figured they might as well turn themselves in. I booked 'em both last night. They copped out to almost all of the burglaries we've had on the east side of town."

"No way!" He laughed. "You've got to be kidding me." And then we both laughed.

"I'm serious. I talked to both of 'em, and they said the same thing. They admitted to twenty burglaries and a bunch of other thefts. My chief loves me."

Irving chuckled. "I'll bet he does. Damn, I wish they'd all do that."

"You mean they don't? You guys have the big rep. That'd never happen here, and I've never seen it happen before."

"Neither have I. And I probably won't for the rest of my career. Or life."

"Hey, Dave."

"Yeah?"

"You guys got any jobs open?"

Two

The Job Is Yours if You Want It!

While in theory the military and the Federal Bureau of Investigation are both agencies of the United States government, the process of *signing up* for each is as different as day and night. To join the Army, Navy, or Marine Corps, one would complete some forms, sign on the dotted line, raise one's hand, then drop 'em, bend over, and spread 'em. Well, maybe not quite that easy.

The long trail of my application to become a Special Agent of the FBI was slightly more complicated. From the time I completed the lengthy, multi-part application form until I was officially offered an appointment as a Special Agent, five years passed. I was completing my second master's program and had pretty much forgotten about the FBI when I received a call from Special Agent Doug Benson, the applicant coordinator in Los Angeles.

"I wanted to see if you were still interested," he said.

I stammered, "Uh, well, yes. I thought you guys had forgotten about me. It's been about five years since I sent in my application. I haven't heard anything. I thought I must have slipped through the cracks."

"Not by any means. We've had a hiring freeze on, and now we're finally able to test and hire some people. I needed to check with you to see if you can update your application and if you still want to go through the testing process."

My first thoughts were about my family and the secure job I had at the police department. I'd been there more than nine years, made sergeant in record time, and was sitting atop the list to be promoted to lieutenant when an opening occurred.

"Let me give you a call back, is that okay? I need to think about it a little," I said.

"No problem. Just let me know as soon as you can. We're starting to set up some testing groups, so I'll need to know by the end of the week."

My wife's reaction was, "Why not? It's what you wanted to do when you finished college and you sent in the application a few years ago. Maybe there's a reason for it to happen now. You might as well go ahead and see what comes of it. If you want to do it, we'll find a way to make it work."

And so I did.

Several weeks later I went to the Los Angeles FBI office on Wilshire Boulevard to begin the testing process. About fifty people were gathered together in a huge bay, all seated behind dark grey, standard government-issue metal desks.

The first part, which involved general aptitude, seemed relatively painless. Since I've always been up on current events and was even a bit of a trivia buff, I left that test feeling pretty good. The second part was a spelling test. A tape recorder blared out words and our job was to spell them properly. I got 49 out of 50 on that part. The third part was a lengthy psychological assessment. I recall a ton of questions being asked, some over and over but in a slightly different way. I had no clue what my result would be on this part, but I tried my best to answer the questions honestly.

A couple of weeks later the applicant coordinator called and asked me to come back down to the Los Angeles FBI office for an interview. "I assume that means I passed the tests," I said, more of a statement than a question.

"Oh yeah, you did fine. Now we need to figure out when you can do the interview." We set up a mutually agreeable date and time.

Benson wanted me to bring my wife along, so we drove to the FBI office that day with mixed feelings. "I don't know what's going to happen with all of this," I remember telling her on the way to the office. "It's very flattering to be considered, but I don't know what I'm going do if they offer me an appointment. I like the job I've got now and we just built a new house. The kids are in school and everything is sailing along pretty well. This is all very flattering, but I don't even know how much they pay. So I'm not sure what to do."

"Don't get the cart ahead of the horse," she remarked. "It hasn't happened yet, so let's not get too excited until we've got a reason to."

I left the interview feeling pretty confident, and my wife Mary Ann felt the same way. "They asked me what I thought about you going in the FBI," she said. "I told them I wanted you to do what you felt was best for you and your family. They seemed to think that was okay."

Several weeks later I received a letter in the mail.

"A national list has been compiled following testing for the position of Special Agent of the Federal Bureau of Investigation. Your ranking is 44 out of 3673 who are currently eligible." I've still got the form letter.

I showed it to my wife, who seemed shocked as she looked at the results and then back at me. "You're in the top two percent. It looks like we've got a decision to make," she said. "What else do they have to do?"

"They've got to do my background investigation and I guess that's it."

"So if you pass that, you're going to be offered an appointment?"

"I think so."

"Are you going to take it?"

"I think so, but I'm not sure."

"Well, you better make sure."

We spent several days discussing our options, and finally decided that if I passed the background check, which amounted to a Top Secret clearance, I'd take the job. I passed and the job was mine if I wanted it.

I did.

Three

Tell the Pilot to Land This Plane!

The morning was clear, bright, and sunny when I left Los Angeles destined for Washington, D.C., filled with more excitement and anticipation than I could ever remember feeling in my life.

Somewhere over the Rockies, our aircraft flew through some rough, stormy weather and began bouncing in and out of turbulent air pockets. I was sitting beside a middle-aged attorney from D.C., who told me he'd been at a conference in Los Angeles all week and was returning home. We chatted a bit, and he was excited to know he was sitting beside a future Special Agent of the Federal Bureau of Investigation. Even though I wasn't one yet.

I'd flown many times, and I'd never been a huge fan of bumpy air. We were sitting toward the back of the plane, which always seems to exacerbate each dip and shake of the aircraft. While I wasn't exactly enjoying myself, the attorney to my right seemed to be beside himself, uncontrollably twisting and fidgeting in his seat and putting a death grip on the armrest. Clearly, he was struggling with the up and down, side-to-side movement of the plane.

The air seemed to smooth out for a few pleasant miles, and I felt relaxed for a while. And then, *wham*! We suddenly hit what must have been a huge air pocket, or some other atmospheric anomaly I couldn't even begin to understand. It felt like we dropped a hundred feet. Which in reality didn't happen, but the abrupt feeling of weightlessness must have been something akin to what astronauts experience in space. It scared the liver out of me.

The man next to me reached over and put on another death grip, this one attached to my left leg! My body froze and tensed.

"We're going down." He was nearly sobbing. "We're all going to die."

"It's okay." I covered his hand with mine, patting it lightly. But I wasn't so sure either of us was okay. "Hang in there, buddy. We're fine." I just wished I could believe myself.

"Stop this plane." His breathing was fast and shallow, and I was worried he might have a heart attack, and that I'd have one right after he did.

"We're all right." I again patted his hand, which was stopping the blood flow in my leg. I was acting confident, but truly was anything but at that moment. While I'd flown many times, turbulence still had the effect of scaring the daylights right out of me.

"No, we're not all right!" he shouted. "We're going to crash. You're important. You're the FBI. Go up there and tell the pilot to land this plane. You're the FBI. He'll listen to you."

I patted his hand once more as the air settled and we returned to having a smooth flight.

Thankfully, he removed his hand.

It was another indication of the presumed power and authority people thought the FBI had: an educated man, an attorney, believed that an FBI agent would have the authority to order the pilot to land an airplane. I wasn't sure if I liked the perception or not, but in years ahead I would come to understand it more and more. And the perception is given even more traction by the manner in which FBI agents are depicted in movies and on television.

"We're good now." I looked toward him and then quickly away.

"Sorry." He breathed calmly again.

"It's fine, don't worry about it."

We popped out of the thickest cloud bank I'd ever flown through and began our descent into Washington National Airport. Suddenly, the vast metropolis of the nation's capital began to appear on my left. We soared over the wide and dark, slowly flowing Potomac River. It looked more like a long lake than a river. I saw the Kennedy Center, the Washington and Lincoln Memorials, and the United States Capitol Building. It was one of the most thrilling days of my life, and I was on the precipice of joining the most prestigious and respected law enforcement agency in the world.

Four

Day One in D.C.

Advertised as a 'fixture' in Washington, D.C. since the turn of the century, the historic Peacock Hotel sat humbly on 7th Street in Washington, D.C., one block north of Pennsylvania Avenue, about a mile west of the United States Capitol building, and a virtual eternity away from Five Star status. As I pulled up in the cab, my first thought was, *In which century was it a fixture?*

Two scruffy, homeless black men in grimy, ragged clothes, one tilting a bottle in a brown paper bag, lounged on the sidewalk in front of the light granite, exhaust-stained, grayish exterior of the hotel. Both men stared expectantly at me as I stepped from the cab and handed the Arab cab driver a twenty-dollar bill. I was dressed in a sharp, well-tailored blue suit, and I'm sure the two grimy-looking men saw me as an easy mark as I hauled my steamer trunk and garment bag into the lobby, ignoring both of them as I passed.

The desk clerk, a middle-aged black woman who was more than slightly heavyset, but quite upbeat and cheerful, wearing a brightly colored, stained Hawaiian mu-mu, greeted me.

"So, honey. You looks like one of them FBI boys."

"Uh, yes ma'am…er, I will be in a couple of days."

"You got a reservation?"

"Yes ma'am. Last name is Klein."

She began sorting through a huge pile of small pieces of paper. "Okay, baby. We gonna take good care of you. We likes you FBI boys here. Yeah baby, getchu a good room."

"Thank you, ma'am." I turned and gazed around the lobby. A couple of older black men sat in faded, tattered chairs behind me, both avidly puffing on foul-smelling cigars, emitting huge plumes of bluish smoke. To my left was a sign proclaiming "Restaurant." No name apparently required.

"Okay, now I need to axe you if you got any ID." I showed her my California driver's license.

"Alright den. I'm putting you in 403. Good room. You'll like it, honey."

"Thank you, ma'am." I was feeling slightly intimidated, which surprised me, because I'd been a cop for years and had never found much that scared me or that I couldn't handle. She handed me a single key attached to a green, diamond-shaped plastic holder.

"Thas' okay, baby." She patted my hand. "We takes good care of our FBI boys here."

"Yes ma'am, uh, thank you." I wasn't entirely sure what "take care of you" meant, but I certainly hoped it didn't mean what I was thinking it did.

The elevator was old European-style. No more than two people could possibly fit into it, so with my baggage it was a tight fit. Which intensified the problem, because as soon as the door closed, the pungent smell of urine and heaven-only-knows-what-else was more than apparent. I didn't even want to think about what the 'heaven-knows-what-else' was. And tried not to.

My room appeared reasonably clean, but small. A thin and worn, faded, orange-colored comforter covered the bed. A small wooden desk and chair were situated against the wall, with a black dial telephone on the desk beside a lamp with a tattered and torn shade. A nine-inch black and white television was firmly bolted onto a rusting metal frame, secured to the wall with a stainless steel chain. The sole window was double-paned, and if closed was presumably thick enough to mute the din of random horns honking, people shouting, and assorted vehicle noises on the street below. It wasn't closed.

I couldn't help but think to myself, *this is where the FBI stays?* I got out of the suit I'd worn on the long flight and started sorting through my clothes. I'd stayed at more than a few questionable places in my lifetime, and this was one place I'd have to add to that list. Since the window was open, the noxious stench of exhaust fumes seeped into my room. The sheer and not-surprisingly torn window cover waved softly in the light breeze coming through. I took a quick look out the window, and the street scene was straight out of Hell's Kitchen. Or Harlem. Or someplace else I'd never been before. And probably didn't want to go.

Slightly down the street to my left, which I assumed was to the west, shone the gleaming, brightly lit theater marquee of proclaiming "XXX 24-7." I assumed that meant all day, and not the name of the film they were featuring. A constellation of interesting characters and vehicles was cruising the street and sidewalk. Several hookers were open for business on the side of the theater, and a garishly dressed pimp stood beside a maroon and silver Lincoln Continental, decked out in his full dress regalia, consisting of a turquoise wide-brimmed hat, trimmed with a fully plumed ostrich feather and a radiant lime leisure suit. They were still in fashion in those days, and Mr. Pimp was wearing his for the maximum visual effect. The nature of his profession was readily apparent.

Several 'normal' cars cruised by and slowed as the hookers approached the passenger side. Two young men in gang colors stood on a street corner, eyeing all the cars that came by. Several cars stopped briefly, an exchange seemed to occur, and the cars sped away. I knew what that meant. I'd spent two years in charge of the Vice and Narcotics Bureau on the department I'd just left. It was clear I was watching drug deals going down left and right, virtually in the shadow of the FBI building, only a block away.

It was getting late and I was hungry, so I decided to avoid the highly intriguing gourmet restaurant downstairs, take a walk, and see a bit of the town. I knew the museums were closed by that time of day, which was fine since I planned to spend the entire next day seeing them. Or as many as I could see in a given space of hours. Little did I know I would only have time to see about one quarter of the museums and monuments. But I also knew there would be time later, on the weekends while I was at the academy.

Five

Hoover's Grip on the FBI

Sleep was a short-lived, fleeting fantasy. With the time change from California to the east coast, I woke up that Sunday at 6:00 a.m. Unfortunately for me, that was East Coast time, which meant it was three in the morning in California. I was excited enough about where I was that I decided to get up and take a couple mile run.

Stepping onto the vacant sidewalk in front of the Peacock Hotel, I stretched and trotted south. The first government building I saw was labeled "U.S. Department of Justice." I slowly ran past it, as the J. Edgar Hoover FBI Building loomed ahead on Pennsylvania Avenue. The tan, modern façade of the FBI Building rose majestically above the street in stark contrast to other government buildings around it. It stood out in a unique way, much like the nature of work that is performed inside.

For nearly fifty years, the FBI and United States Department of Justice occupied the Justice Department building together. It was something of an unholy marriage of the investigative and prosecutorial arms of the federal government, made even more problematic by the popularity of Hoover, the prominent face of the FBI. But it made sense, because it put the FBI in direct contact with the people in the government who would provide legal advice for, and ultimately prosecute, the cases which would gain great prominence in the history of the country.

Americans in the 1960s and 1970s could easily identify the Director, but very few could identify the top law enforcement official in the country, the Attorney

General of the United States. One exception, of course, would be Bobby Kennedy, who became an avowed enemy of Hoover in the 1960s. Attorneys General, however, typically labored in anonymity outside the capital city, or as Hoover came to call it, "Seat of Government."

The FBI Director was not a Cabinet member like the Attorney General, but few would deny his prominence on the American scene. Hoover was the penultimate politician and promoter of the organization he built, literally from the ground up. His public relations skills were sharply tuned into demonstrating the awesome power and investigative abilities of his personal fiefdom, with thousands of agents and support personnel. He sought and received every imaginable favor from the American press corps and was a close friend with Jack Anderson, the most well-known Washington pundit of the era.

Hoover built the FBI from a corrupt organization in the 1920s to the well-oiled investigative machine it remains today. He was the consummate dictator, leading by fear and intimidation, and the infamous 'dossiers' he secretly maintained on prominent Americans were legendary.

The stories about Hoover's power and authority are equally fabled, as is the climate of fear and intimidation he created everywhere he went. Few agents who were in the bureau before he died in 1972 can't recite a personal story about an encounter with the Director. Hoover had several qualities which seemingly approached mania. He would not tolerate an agent who didn't fit the 'Bureau Image.' If an agent was too heavy, he could face the prospect of immediate dismissal. No questions asked.

I recalled a story Dave Irving, our resident agent, told me at an area investigator's meeting a few months before I received my appointment as a Special Agent.

Ralph Simmons was an agent in the early 1970s. Assigned to the New York office of the FBI, Special Agent Simmons had slowly gained weight over his twenty years in the bureau and was at least thirty pounds over his 'bureau weight.' While visiting headquarters one day, Simmons had a meeting scheduled with Hoover about a case he was working on.

"Well, Ralph," Hoover said as he looked over his reading glasses and across his desk, which was roughly the size of a Carnival cruise ship. "You've done a good job on this case. I appreciate all the hard work you've put in. And the results show."

"Thank you, sir." Simmons breathed a sigh of relief. He knew any little flaw in his investigation or what he said in reports could have rung the death knell on his career. And he was only five years away from retirement. Hoover was known to send agents to outlying offices such as Butte, Montana, if he didn't feel they were getting the job done properly. Or would fire an agent on the spot.

"Now," Hoover growled, "there's something else we need to talk about."

Simmons felt a sharp pang of anxiety strike him like a bolt of lightning had pierced his brain. "Y-yes sir," he stammered. "And what's that, Mr. Hoover?" The anxiety suddenly hit him in the bladder and he had an urge to run immediately to the Director's personal bathroom. His blood pressure, already too high, shot up about a hundred points on the systolic end.

"You've put on some weight, Ralph." Hoover removed his glasses, staring at Simmons. "You've been in this organization long enough to know I don't like that."

"Uh…" Simmons sucked in his expanding gut, which was straining his vest. Agents *always* wore their 'Sunday best' when having a meeting with the Director. "Yes sir. You're right. I have. I'm really sorry."

"Sorry doesn't feed the bulldog, Ralph." Hoover's eyes were glaring, and his face was twisted into an appearance of anger. "I want to see you here in six months, and I want that weight off of you. I'm going to tell your boss to put you on the fat boy program. Do you understand me?"

Simmons could tell the Director was serious. He was *always* serious.

"Yes sir." Simmons was dismissed. He stood and left the room, immediately thinking about what he'd be doing in his next career. His knees felt like they were made of soft rubber, and each one was in business for itself. Somehow he got past Hoover's secretary, reached the walnut-paneled hallway, and put both hands and his head against the wall. An Assistant Director was approaching.

"You okay, Ralph?"

"Oh…uh…yes sir. I'm fine." Simmons was anything but. His career was passing before his eyes, and he wasn't sure if he could make it as a private investigator.

"Did you get yelled at?" the AD said.

"No, sir…" Simmons wasn't sure what to say. "Mr. Hoover just thinks I'm too fat."

The AD looked at him. "He's right, Ralph. You have put on some weight. We've got an image to uphold in this organization and you're not cutting the mustard."

That comment raised Simmons' blood pressure to pre-heart attack status.

"Yes, sir." Simmons walked down the hall as the AD went into the inner sanctum for some important meeting with the boss.

For the next several months, Simmons couldn't think about anything other than his weight and his upcoming meeting with the Director. And so he sought refuge in his favorite comfort. Food. And gained yet another ten pounds. He wasn't a runner or workout fanatic, and had very little self-discipline in anything other than the top-notch investigations he had produced for many years. But he knew that simply wasn't enough. *You can put together the best case in the world*, he thought to himself while bemoaning his fate one afternoon in the office. *But if you don't fit the 'bureau image' in every way, you might find yourself without a job.* Simmons and every other agent in the bureau *knew* that was true.

But what to do? He could feel the additional pounds in his clothes. And knew he was eating even more to manage his stress. He functioned, but barely. The quality of his work began to suffer. His mind was obsessed with his upcoming meeting with The Director.

Several weeks later, Simmons was called into the office of his Special Agent in Charge (SAC). "Ralph, Mr. Hoover called me today," his boss said. Simmons' heart rate shot up to 120 beats per minute. He could feel his face flush, and his body temperature probably rose a few degrees as well. "He wants to know what's going on with that big case of yours and I wasn't sure exactly where things were. He chewed my ass out and told me he wants to see you in D.C. on Friday." Simmons was ready to call an ambulance for what he knew was a heart attack.

"Yes sir." Simmons could barely breathe. The front of his head felt like small gremlins were pounding it with huge hammers. Like a bell. He knew he couldn't lose forty pounds in a few days, and again started thinking about where he would be working the following week. *Maybe being a PI won't be that bad,* he thought as he walked out of his SAC's office.

On Thursday of that week, Simmons went to a local Goodwill store. It was his only hope. He knew what he had to do. There was no other choice.

At a fever pitch, Simmons searched through the huge rack of donated suits. And then he found what he was searching for. It was perfect.

The next morning, after a red-eye flight to Washington, D.C., Simmons donned his new acquisition, which literally hung off his body like a tent from Omar's shop in Lebanon. And promptly at 8:00 a.m., Simmons arrived at the hallowed office of The Director of the FBI.

"Good morning, Ralph." Hoover's secretary scanned him carefully. "Have you lost some weight?"

"Uh…yes, ma'am." Simmons tugged on his loosely fitting vest, pulling it over his gut. "Thank you."

A buzzer on her desk beckoned Simmons into the walnut-paneled office of Mr. Hoover.

"Mornin' sir." Simmons entered, noticing the Director sitting behind a large pile of files on his desk.

"Good morning, Ralph." Hoover glared over his reading glasses, removed them and stared at Simmons. "Jesus Christ, son!" he bellowed. "You *did* listen to me. Ralph, you've lost quite a bit of weight."

"Thank you sir, I did the best I could." Simmons adjusted the huge suit coat, not admitting he hadn't lost a pound. He knew it was all about image, and if that was what the boss wanted to think, he'd be more than happy to let him think it.

"I'll send an Airtel to your SAC and tell him to get you off the fat boy program, Ralph. Good job."

The meeting with Hoover lasted no more than a half hour, focused only on the investigation he was heading, and was much more pleasant than the first one.

Ralph went on to gain even more weight and to retire happily from the FBI about five years later.

It seemed I couldn't stop running that morning, probably fueled by excitement from seeing all of the sights of Washington, D.C., and even perhaps subconsciously motivated by avoiding the problems faced by Ralph Simmons many years before I entered on duty. My excitement of being in the capital city of the United States turned a couple miles into five or six.

Six

Swearing In as a Special Agent

Finally, Monday morning arrived. It seemed like an eternity had passed, but the most important day of my career was here.

I donned a starched, laundered shirt, a red patterned tie, and my best blue suit. I did a quick check in the mirror and thought I looked presentable. My intuitive senses told me it was important to *look the part*, again thinking of the omnipresent image of Efrem Zimbalist, Jr., and even Jimmy Stewart in *The FBI Story*. Several months of running before my arrival had trimmed my body down to a solid 205 pounds, which was a good weight on my 6'2" frame. After a final look in the mirror, I straightened my tie and got my gear ready to haul over to the FBI Building.

A uniformed guard at the FBI Building, sharply clad in a crisp white shirt and dark blue pants, reviewed a list, found my name, and looked carefully at my California driver's license to ensure the person on the list was the same person who was about to be admitted to the building.

It was seven thirty when I hauled my trunk and clothes bag into a small, well-appointed auditorium on the lower level. A few others had arrived before me. Once I secured my baggage, I introduced myself to them and others as they arrived. It was exciting to discover where everyone was from and what they did in their pre-bureau lives. My first impression was positive. The quality of the people in my class was unlike any collection of individuals I had ever been around. And the diversity of the group was equally interesting. It appeared we had eight women, several blacks and Hispanics, and the rest were pretty much just like me. I couldn't wait to meet the rest of my future classmates.

At precisely 8:00 a.m., a tall and strikingly handsome man, wearing an obviously expensive suit, strode earnestly onto the stage. He stepped to the podium, asking everyone to find a seat. Which wasn't difficult in an auditorium designed to seat about five hundred. It was all very impressive, exceeding what I had imagined it would be.

"Good morning, ladies and gentlemen," he began after we all had positioned ourselves in padded, comfortable, royal blue cushioned seats. I immediately noticed the FBI seal on the face of the podium, a United States flag and dark blue FBI flag to his left and right. The curtain that covered the rear wall of the stage was royal blue, with impressive, dark wood highlights at the top and both sides. It was impressive, and probably a little intimidating. The room was so quiet you could easily hear a mouse fart, but the chances of finding a mouse in that building was pretty improbable.

"My name is Tom Jensen, and I will be your field counselor during your training at the FBI Academy." I had no clue what a field counselor was. He spoke slowly and deliberately, obviously reading from a script he'd brought to the podium. His hair was dark brown, stylish, neatly trimmed over his ears, and he sported an equally well-trimmed, dark mustache that was perfectly cut to the corners of his mouth. The suit he wore was an expensive one, a dark shade of green, with subtle stripes in a Scottish kilt pattern, making me think, *is this how the FBI dresses?* I didn't know if I could ever afford a suit of such quality. *Maybe you make enough as an agent to dress like that.*

"Let me tell you a little about how the day will go for you," he continued in a deadpan tone. "In a moment, you will meet your academy counselor. Following that, you will be sworn in as Special Agents of the Federal Bureau of

Investigation by our Assistant Director. We will then take care of some administrative duties, get pictures taken for your credentials, and board the bus for the FBI Academy in Quantico. That should be an hour drive, traffic permitting. Then we'll unload and have lunch in the cafeteria. From there, we'll head to our classroom, where we'll all meet after lunch. Any questions?"

Jensen looked around the auditorium, saw no hands raised, and continued. "I'd now like to introduce you to Supervisory Special Agent Sam Batterson, who will be your academy counselor for the duration of your training in Quantico."

All eyes in the auditorium looked to the left as a nondescript man strode toward the podium. He was less than six feet tall with a sturdy, athletic build, and wore a plain grey three-piece suit. His manner seemed much more relaxed than Jensen's. "Good morning, ladies and gentlemen. On behalf of Assistant Director of the FBI Academy, Dr. Kenneth Joseph, I'd like to welcome each and every one of you to your first day in the FBI."

My first thought upon seeing Batterson was, *I like this guy*. He was plain looking, not pretentious in any way, and seemed to convey an air of calm confidence. A man's man. Jensen seemed like the stereotype of an FBI agent, maybe someone who took himself too seriously. That opinion would soon change, however.

Batterson quickly explained some details about the different phases of training at the academy, and that some of the people in the auditorium would not be around for graduation. "You are the most select group of law enforcement officers in the world. But even though that is the case, we lose between ten and twenty percent of the agents in each of our New Agent Classes."

I looked around the auditorium, thinking I might not want to get too close to anyone, because they might not be with our class too long.

"The training you will receive is the best in the world, as is the equipment and technology," Batterson said. "We will spend thousands of dollars on each and every one of you. We expect you to graduate from the academy as fully prepared Special Agents of the FBI. It is our commitment to you that we will do the best job possible to ensure your success. But a lot of that depends on you."

I was starting to feel a little queasy inside. It was terrifying to think I could be one of the new agents who wouldn't make it through the sixteen weeks of training.

Batterson spoke a little more, explaining some of the routine we'd face at the academy, and then said, "Now, I'd like to introduce Dr. Kenneth Joseph, the Assistant Director in Charge of the FBI Academy."

Dr. Joseph, a tall man in a dark grey suit, walked sternly to the podium. He scanned the class and said, "Please stand and raise your right hand."

Everyone in the audience stood in unison.

"Repeat after me. I, say your name, promise to enforce the laws of the United States of America in an equal manner, without prejudice or preference, to maintain the highest ethical standards of the Federal Bureau of Investigation, to live my life in a manner befitting a Special Agent of the FBI, and to uphold the credo of the FBI, 'Fidelity, Bravery and Integrity.' So help me God." He looked up from his script. "Please lower your hands. Congratulations. You are now Special Agents of the FBI." Dr. Joseph turned from the podium and walked off the stage. We'd never see him again.

Batterson returned to the podium. "Let me offer my congratulations as well. You all know the selection process you went through to be in this room. We want only the best and we know we've got that in each of you. I'm told there were well over ten thousand people who applied to be FBI agents this past recruiting cycle. Of those, less than half qualified after all the testing. This class is very high on the list of those qualified and approved."

From the auditorium, we were led through the halls of the J. Edgar Hoover FBI Building. Pictures were taken, credentials were signed, temporary badges were issued, and in a couple of fast-paced hours we were winging our way south on Interstate 395 toward the FBI Academy.

I had served my country in the United States Navy on submarines during two separate tours in Vietnam. I'd finished near the top of my class in college and was first in my police academy class. I was proud of that, but now I was a Special Agent of the FBI. I had never been prouder of anything in my life.

Seven

Day One at the FBI Academy

The unmistakable signs of fall in Virginia were apparent well before we got to the *Marine Base – Quantico* exit from Interstate 395. Our drive down in two busses was impeded by light traffic on the Beltway and south through Springfield, Manassas, and Dumfries. And probably some other exits I don't remember.

A brilliant display of multi-colored oak and elm trees greeted us as we exited to a road heading west toward the FBI Academy. Our driver announced, "Seven more miles and we're there, folks."

The thickly wooded landscape was in stark contrast to California, and certainly my home state of Colorado. The gold, rust-colored, and bright orange leaves on thousands of trees that framed parts of the road were a stunning sight as the bus wound its way toward the academy. It had been many years since I'd seen trees changing colors in the Rockies, but I'd never seen anything like this autumn spectacular.

We cruised past perfectly manicured rifle ranges, huge ammunition bunkers, and other buildings associated with the training of Marine Corps combat officers. More than a few men, clad in either Marine Corps jogging togs or grey and blue shirts and shorts were trudging along on a path beside the asphalt roadway. And suddenly it came into view. Looming over the treetops was the first building of the FBI Academy. We rounded a curve, saw some pistol ranges on the right, and more buildings.

Two huge dorm buildings stood like tan brick sentinels in the midst of more trees than I could imagine being in one place. As we turned into the rear of the cafeteria access and pulled over near a loading dock, I saw an airplane on the right and, near the plane, a Huey helicopter of Vietnam fame. *This place is the real deal,* I thought. The vastness of the buildings and the landscape was incredible, and I was sure I'd only seen the tip of the iceberg.

But most impressive to me were the buildings. Constructed of tan bricks and mortar, the FBI Academy seemed to go on forever. My dad, a brick contractor, would have reveled in looking over such an impressive array of structures and the complex brickwork incorporated within. I silently hoped the day would come when he would see it. I was very proud, and knew he was pleased with me for achieving the pinnacle of my profession. We'd talked on the phone before I left California, and even though he didn't come right out and say it, I knew he was very proud of his son for being hired by the world famous FBI. I really wanted him to see the academy someday, but to my disappointment he never would.

In a flurry of activity, we offloaded our bags, hauled them into a long hallway, and headed up the stairs to the cafeteria for lunch.

The line was short and the food was tempting. But the biggest treat was walking out of the food line and into the dining hall itself. "Oh my God." I stopped as I carried my tray through the doorway and looked up and around the huge dining hall. "This is incredible."

Jim Mason, my roommate-to-be, was in line ahead of me and hit the brakes like I had. "Look at this," he said. He paused briefly, scanned the vastness of the dining hall, and turned to me. "Have we died and gone to heaven or what?" We both headed for the salad bar, which was nearly as sumptuous as the food line.

"Ahhh, man," I commented. "If I knew this salad bar was here, I wouldn't have loaded up on this fattening stuff." My tray was filled with tantalizing, but high-calorie chow. "I really need to spend a little more time eating salads than all that junk. Gotta stay within weight limits."

Huge windows around the cafeteria provided a panoramic view of both dormitories, a grassed, park-like area between them, and the three-level FBI Academy library building. Above the windows, flags of every state were positioned in alphabetical order. I quickly located my duel home states of Colorado and California and glanced around at the remaining states. "This is impressive," I whispered to Mason, trying to not look like too much of a tourist.

Seated at plain, rectangular tables were groups of men and women, clad in either red polo shirts or dress shirts with ties. The red-shirted group would prove to be law enforcement officers from around the nation and world, all of whom were attending the FBI National Academy.

Sometime in the 1930s, J. Edgar Hoover came to the realization that most law enforcement officers in the United States were hired and went to work on the street with little or no training for the job. Hoover saw an opportunity to partner with law enforcement throughout the country, and began the FBI National Training Academy. Securing government funding, Hoover paid for officers from agencies around the country to travel to Washington, D.C. for a basic law enforcement training academy which encompassed eight weeks. Included in the training was an opportunity to learn about the law, tactics, arrest control, and the proper use of firearms. No one knows how many officers were ultimately saved by this training, but most of the officers then returned to their agencies and conducted training for their own officers. And so the influence of the FBI spread in a very positive way. Many officers in American law enforcement felt a debt of gratitude to the FBI for enhancing their professional standing.

Eight

Lunch and a Dose of Reality

Our class gravitated toward tables that were occupied by men and women in the red shirts. As we found our seats and set our trays down, one of the grizzled officers commented, "Well, look here. A new class of baby agents!" The men sitting around him chuckled in appreciation. I'd never heard the term before, and snickered right along with them.

"Yup," one of our group retorted. "We're the rookies." Our class had all found seats and started digging into the different carbohydrate-loaded choices we made.

"Where you from?" asked a man who appeared to be in his forties and was seated directly across from me.

I replied, "Most recently California, but I'm really a native of Colorado."

"No kidding! Where in Colorado?"

"Denver area."

"I'm with Denver P.D."

"Really. All right. I grew up in Englewood and went to college in Denver."

"What school?"

"University of Denver."

"Did you know Cy Hansen or Lee Dishlacoff?"

"Sure, had them both as professors. But that was a long time ago." Having made an immediate connection, we talked about several other Denver P.D. officers I had gone to school with, most of whom he didn't know. We also talked about my experience on the police department in California.

"What made you give that up and come in the bureau?" he asked.

"Oh, probably a lot of things. I actually wanted to go into the FBI when I was sixteen and used to watch *The Untouchables* on television."

"That wasn't the FBI, though."

"I know that now, but I didn't know it then. I thought Elliott Ness was an FBI agent, not with the ATF."

"So, basically you screwed up and now you're in the FBI!"

We both laughed.

"Yeah, pretty much," I said. "Actually, when I finished college, I went down to the FBI office in Denver. I didn't know what their requirements were, but I was always intrigued by the bureau, I suppose. However, I was quickly disabused of that idea when they told me I needed to get some experience doing something after college. I had the job in California locked up and decided I'd head there. And pretty much forgot about going in the bureau until I was working on a master's degree in Public Administration at the University of Southern California."

"Was O.J. playing ball there then?"

"Nah, he finished quite a few years before I was there. I was actually heading toward a police chief's job somewhere, if not on my own department. But several guys from the FBI office in L.A. were going to school with me and we got to be friends of sorts. I guess they liked me and a few of them talked me into filling out an application. So here I am."

"Lucky you!"

"We'll see about that. I'm glad to be here, but I'm also pretty nervous about whether or not I'm going to make it through the academy."

"Hey," he snorted. "Look around a little bit." I scanned the groups of new agents sitting at other tables.

"The FBI isn't the same FBI that most of us old timers are used to seeing."

"Really? How so?"

"Well…" He paused for effect. "Most of us aren't too impressed with the quality of the new agents they seem to be getting. In Hoover's day, it was all men and none of them were wimps. Now, this guy Judge Webster seems to be hiring some midgets in trying to be diverse."

I couldn't help but burst out laughing, and bumped a classmate next to me, who wasn't one of that select group he described. "Did you hear what he said?" And then told him.

"The FBI was the premier law enforcement agency in the world when Hoover ran it," my new friend continued. "He was a little crazy, but he built a well-respected outfit. You were a cop, you know what I'm talking about."

"Well, yeah. Obviously, the FBI has a big reputation, and I think that was part of the attraction for me. Other than going to school with a few agents, I really didn't know that many. We had a resident agent in my town who I got to know a bit, plus a few of his fellow agents at our monthly investigators meetings. But that was pretty much it."

"Same here. We all got to know some agents, and developed a working relationship with a few. Most of us respected 'em, but now, things seem to be changing. I'm not sure if it's for the better either."

"How's that?"

"Start with this place. The academy is basically bullshit. It's a big show, but no substance for you guys. The place is great, it looks good, but the training you get is pretty useless. You're lucky, you've been a cop and you know what assholes people can be on the street. You'll be surprised at how much that's going to help you."

"That's good. I hoped it would, but I didn't know for sure."

"You're gonna be light-years ahead of everyone in your class. They take accountants and teachers, lawyers, and whatever else, and try to make them real agents in four months. Can't be done. I've talked to a ton of ex-cops like you who were getting ready to graduate. And they're scared shitless about going on the street with some of these people who don't have a clue what they're about to face in the real world. The only new agents who get it are guys like you and the ones with military experience. The old guard in the bureau thinks the academy is the be-all and end-all, but most of us who have gone through a police academy are far better prepared to face our jobs than these kids."

"Interesting," I said and rubbed my chin.

"And the worst part is, they say, 'We're the FBI and this is how we do things.' They won't listen to anyone else, and it's going to catch up with them one of these days. Good training is what law enforcement's all about. These people have no clue what that means. It's like training for the sake of training, but nothing that's going to help you much in your first field office. I worked in our academy at Denver for a couple of years. We were constantly changing things to make it better for our new officers. These people are going to give you a full week of training in some useless crap like first aid and fingerprinting. Photography!" He sneered. "They waste a ton of time back here and refuse to train agents in street survival skills. You guys will be able to shoot a beetle off a target at fifty yards, but they'll never give you a clue when you can shoot. Or should shoot."

He started to collect his utensils, preparing to head back to his own classes. "It's basically a waste of at least three or four weeks which you could be using to learn how to survive on the street. It's all for show. They've got this ancient 'Hogan's Alley' complex which was all right for agents back in the thirties, but this isn't the thirties anymore. The old days are long gone and they just won't change from what they were doing to train agents back then.

"Look P.J., you know this, you were a cop. We're dealing with bad-ass groups like the SLA who kidnapped Patty Hearst, and big-time drug cartels. These bad boys aren't afraid to shoot it out with anyone. They don't give a damn if you shout 'FBI.' They'll turn on you in a heartbeat and put one right through your head. Your agents are hitting the streets with six shooters, and you're going up against semiautomatic pistols and rifles, M16s. There's some bad dudes out there and you're one of the few lucky ones in your class who knows that. I'd hate to be you. When you're done here and you hit the street in your first office, you'll see exactly what I'm talking about."

He gave me a pat on the shoulder as he and several of his classmates picked up their trays and prepared to head back to class. "Good luck, buddy."

"Thanks." I really couldn't think of anything else to say. I hoped he was wrong, but my instincts told me he wasn't.

Nine

Origins of the Academy

The genesis of what would become the FBI Academy in Quantico, Virginia, came from the most unlikely of all possible sources.

Charles Arthur "Pretty Boy" Floyd was one of the more infamous and notorious gangsters from the 1930s, when bank robbers and other ne'er-do-wells freely roamed the Midwest.

The story of the academy began in Kansas City, Missouri in June of 1933. Floyd and several armed cohorts confronted three police officers and an FBI agent who were escorting a recaptured bank robber by the name of Frank Nash. On arrival at Union Station, the officers approached an awaiting car and were ambushed by the bandits, who opened fire with automatic weapons. Nash was killed in the ensuing firefight, as were the three officers and Special Agent Ray Caffrey of the FBI.

Prior to what has since been named "The Kansas City Massacre," FBI agents were not authorized to carry guns or make arrests. Their function up to the shootout in Kansas City was deemed to be strictly 'investigative.' Public outcry followed, and emergency legislation was passed by Congress. FBI agents were finally given the authority to make arrests and to carry weapons for the first time.

Bureau agents had been undergoing informal, on the job training since the early 1920s, but training of agents was not formalized until 1929 with the launching of a training school for agents in Washington, D.C. Classroom training in a myriad of topics such as fingerprinting, investigative techniques, law, and evidence collection prepared agents for what they'd deal with in the field. Except for training in firearms, which they were not authorized to carry, although some were rumored to have done so.

When J. Edgar Hoover sought approval from Congress to arm his agents, the public was supportive and thousands of letters were sent to congressmen. The measure had unanimous support and passed swiftly in Congress. But then a problem emerged: where to conduct marksmanship training? With the academy housed in the U.S. Post Office in Washington, a safe place out of the population center was needed immediately.

The problem was solved in 1934, courtesy of an unlikely benefactor, the U.S. Marine Corps. For two weeks of their training, agents would stay in barracks and use one of the many firing ranges on the Marine base at Quantico. A qualified pool of instructors was readily available, and the bureau began training new agents, as well as newly-armed agents in the field.

Things moved quickly. Responding to a national commission's mandate for conducting police training, in 1935 the FBI launched what was then called the "Police Training School," the forerunner of today's FBI National Academy. Higher-level police professionals from around the country received training in investigative and scientific techniques. Practical exercises were offered, as were classes in management principles and firearms. The goal of the school is the same today as it was in the 1930s: for the graduates to return to their agencies and share the information they'd learned. The theory behind all of this was that the level of professionalism would rise in the police ranks across the country.

As the 1930s progressed, it became apparent the FBI needed a central place to instruct and house the growing number of police officers and newly-appointed special agents it was training. A primary need, however, was a firing range. The first classroom building opened on the main section of the Marine Corps base in 1940. The FBI Academy was born.

The original building was expanded in the 1960s, but it still wasn't enough. Eight officers or agents would share a single dorm room. The lack of classroom space limited the size of training classes. The firing range was a bumpy bus ride away. In a word, the FBI needed new facilities to match the vision it had for world-class law enforcement training. Again, the Marine Corps obliged, loaning the FBI 385 acres of land on the eastern outskirts of the base.

In 1965, with the proposed building site identified, Congress approved funding and authorized the construction of a new complex for FBI training at Quantico. Millions of dollars were allocated to the project, and a throng of architects and consultants convened to develop the elaborate plans.

Fraught with cost overruns, the ambitious project took years to complete. Finally, in May 1972, the new and modernized, vastly expanded FBI Academy was opened. The upgrade was an epic improvement over the previous diminutive facility. Included were over two dozen modern classrooms with all of the latest technology. Twin seven-story dormitories dominated the landscape. A one thousand-seat auditorium, expansive dining room with double serving lines, a full-sized gymnasium, swimming pool, a fully equipped library, and new firing ranges completed the spectacular venue.

Other enhancements included specialized classrooms for training in forensic science, several identification labs, more than a dozen darkrooms, and simulated city and crime scene rooms for practical exercises. It was unquestionably the most far-reaching effort ever conceived to advance the cause of professionalizing law enforcement training.

In later years, the bureau expanded the facility with a mock town on campus called "Hogan's Alley." In the 1980s and 1990s, buildings were added for engineering research, and to house agents from the Critical Incident Response Group, which includes the FBI's Hostage Rescue Team. In later years other buildings were added, significant among which is a laboratory building that enables the FBI to continue its pioneering work in the forensic sciences.

But the man whose broad vision created the structures which house agents in training, regrettably did not live to see the dedication of the building. J. Edgar Hoover died only days before the facility opened.

When Jim Mason and I hauled our luggage into our room after lunch, the first matter of importance was figuring out who got which bed. I looked at Mason, then at the two beds, both of which were unmade and had folded sheets, a bedcover, and pillow sitting neatly in the middle of the mattresses.

"Doesn't matter to me," he said graciously.

The cop in me said to get as far away from the door as possible, so I chose the bed against the wall separating us from the bathroom. The room was stark, but functional. The walls were painted an alabaster white. Two unmade single beds were placed on each side of the main room with a desk and chair separating them. A single incandescent light above that desk supplied the room with its primary illumination. Against the opposite wall at the foot of one twin bed was another, identical desk. Both desks were built of solid pressed board and covered with laminated wood. To the left of that was a large, similarly laminated armoire, and a door opposite the closet-like structure which led to a bathroom. No artwork on the walls. It was clearly not intended to resemble a room in a motel. However, a single tall window afforded a view onto the forest to the west of the dorms.

I threw the luggage on my new bed and said, "It looks like we've got a little time to put our stuff away before our first class."

"Yeah," Mason replied. "But it's going to take us a while to figure out where the classroom is. From what I've seen, this place looks like we have to find our way through a maze."

"Good point. Let's minimize the organizing and maximize the time to figure out where we're supposed to be."

"Sounds like a plan. We've got plenty of time to get this stuff put away, but I don't want to be late for our first class session." I could tell that Mason was going to be a roommate I could get along with very well.

Ten

A Class on Bureau History

Trying to explain our first week at the FBI Academy would be about like describing the national weather for a week in the United States. We went through a hurricane of activities followed by a blizzard of paperwork, and spent every single night pouring down beer after dinner. It just seemed like a stressful week to many of us, and so we sought our own means to cope.

We quickly learned that Sam Batterson's role with our class would be more administrative than hands-on. While we wouldn't see him much during our training, he explained he would be in the background taking care of a myriad of administrative tasks for our class. Some of those would begin that Monday afternoon.

Tom Jensen would be the person having day-to-day contact with us, even to the extent he would live in a dorm room on the same floor as we did. In that way, he would effectively function in a role similar to that of a Resident Assistant for a college dorm. Little did he know how challenging that role would become in the ensuing weeks.

After lunch Jim Mason and I, along with the rest of our classmates, managed to navigate our way through the labyrinth of so-called 'gerbil tubes' which connected the many buildings comprising the brick-and-mortar portion of the academy. We quickly gained an appreciation for the vastness of the edifice built as a monument to J. Edgar Hoover. One morning of that first week would be devoted to a comprehensive tour of the most astonishing educational facility I had ever seen. It wasn't hard to see why they called it the "West Point of Law Enforcement." But we would eventually come to realize that term was accurate in a physical, but not necessarily educational, sense.

Batterson and Jensen were both in the classroom when we arrived and found our designated places. One of eight rooms in the classroom building used for New Agent trainees, each room boasted rows of curved countertops and attached seats, and the rows were tiered above one another in a mini-amphitheater setting. There were five rows for seating, meaning the classroom could accommodate about fifty people for lectures. Our names had already been printed on a piece of paper and affixed in alphabetical order on the front of the narrow counter where we would sit for sixteen weeks. The overall appearance of the classroom seemed to be more utilitarian and functional than impressive.

Batterson was at the podium and began passing out what would turn out to be an avalanche of forms for us to review and sign. Included in this was a thick packet of rules for the academy, neatly tucked into a notebook with the FBI seal. Among many requirements in those instructions was one clearly spelling out the rules concerning alcohol consumption in the academy buildings. It was permissible at the academy's Boardroom, but no alcoholic beverages were to be allowed in the dorm rooms. I could certainly understand that, but would soon learn how that restriction was almost universally ignored.

I also remember being surprised at another single page form we were required to sign. This document, titled "Pre-Publication Approval," spelled out how any future book or article which an agent would author, whether it involved the FBI or not, had to be approved by the FBI before it could be published. I was a bit shocked when I reviewed this requirement, wondering how the FBI could ignore the main provision of the First Amendment to the Constitution, which spelled out *Free Speech.* My impression was we had no choice but to sign the form, which I did, but always felt I had a gun pointed at me when I signed and dated such a seemingly restrictive piece of paper.

Once Batterson completed his task of passing out the paperwork and Jensen collected it, Batterson looked out at the class and said, "There are several things I want you to understand about your training at the FBI Academy. It has been refined for many years, and we believe it is the best available in the world. We are training FBI agents, not police officers. We expect you to leave this academy as fully trained FBI agents, ready to face the challenges in your first field office. You will receive orders in your twelfth week, and you will have some say about where you would like to go." He paused. "But that doesn't mean you're going there. Some people claim there is a gorilla in the transfer unit at headquarters that is trained to throw darts at a map of the United States. Trust me—your name will soon be on one of those darts."

After making several other comments, Batterson was about to release the class for the rest of the afternoon when he seemed to remember one more thing. "By the way. You all need to head up to the academy store and buy your range clothes and gym suits. You'll be using both this week or next. When you're done with that, you'll have a little bit of time to look around, but on Wednesday I'll have a staff member give you a complete tour of the buildings and what occurs in each one. I think you'll be impressed. I realize it can be confusing to find your way around at first, but you'll figure it out. Just so you know, there is a legend that a New Agent trainee is still wandering around lost somewhere in this maze of buildings. So if you happen to find him, please return him to his owner. I might also suggest you get out on Hoover Road and get some running done. I realize most of you have been running before you arrived here, but you all need to eat well and stay in shape, because we're going to put you through your paces in the physical training portion of the academy."

The next three days were devoted to the things Batterson had told us would happen, and much more. Our tour of the facility took an entire morning. When we were done inside and outside, we probably had walked three miles. We were shown the ranges and the armory, and issued our brand-new Smith and Wesson .38 revolvers. Those of us who had weapons with us, which I did, were required to turn them in to the supervisor of the weapons storage room. It was from there we would check out our service revolver each time we went to the range. We had dull but important sessions explaining our pay and health benefits, then we were given a choice of several plans which would cover ourselves and our family, if we had one. Not everyone in the class did.

Our first session in the gym included an orientation to the equipment available and what our requirements for physical training would be. I had been running for several months before arriving at the academy, so I didn't think running two miles in less than sixteen minutes would be problematic. However, there would also be a minimum number of pull-ups and push-ups, plus a short but grueling obstacle course to complete in less than twenty seconds. I decided I needed to put in some work at the weight room to improve my upper body strength. We all needed to do a minimum of six overhand pull-ups, and I could only do two.

Finally on that Friday afternoon, we had our first official lecture of our academy training.

"J. Edgar Hoover was one of my heroes, and I don't care what's been said about the man since he died. He built and ran the greatest investigative agency in the world. Mr. Hoover is an icon in this country and he was a great American." Supervisory Special Agent (SSA) George Young looked up and stared at the class in an intimidating manner.

Young had walked into the classroom to complete and total silence, placed his notes on the podium, and scanned the class before beginning his lecture on the "History and Culture of the FBI." He appeared to be about fifty years old, and a man J. Edgar Hoover would want as a representative of his well-oiled machine.

Tall and trim and dressed in a deep blue, perfectly-cut suit, Young could have easily filled in for Efrem Zimbalist, Jr. on the Sunday television episode of *The FBI*. His dark hair was exquisitely trimmed at the back and on the sides, with only a hint of grey on the sideburns. Young was literally the 'poster boy' for the image J. Edgar Hoover sought to develop and preserve in his agents.

"Mr. Hoover was twenty-nine years old when the president appointed him to head what was then called 'The Bureau of Investigation.' It was a small, corrupt, and ineffective organization. He was an attorney and a graduate of one of the best law schools in America. He was young, but he was a well-regarded prosecutor with the Department of Justice, serious and dedicated, and probably one of the greatest administrators American government has ever seen." He looked up briefly from his prepared text.

I glanced over at my roommate as I busily took notes on Young's lecture. Mason raised his eyebrows and grimaced, and we both knew that meant the lecture was making it hard for him to keep his eyes open. However, the apprehension Young instilled in each of us unmistakably made it a good idea to stay awake. His voice was flat and he spoke in a monotone as he read from a script he'd clearly prepared and had undoubtedly used many times before. He reviewed the events in the history of the FBI from the 1930s to the present, and despite his dry delivery the subject matter became surprisingly interesting to me. I took notes furiously, assuming everything he said would be on a test at some point in the future.

"I've been a Special Agent of the Federal Bureau of Investigation for twenty-five years. Those years have been the best years of my life." He paused and looked out at the class. "There is nothing in my life I have been prouder of than being in the FBI, and I hope all of you feel the same way. This is not a job. It's an honor to serve as a Special Agent of the FBI, and if any of you don't feel the same way, you should not be here.

"In the next two weeks, I will expect you to have read *The FBI*, and to have completed a report on that book. There are plenty of copies available in the library, where each of you will check one out. We will discuss it in my next class." He collected his notes, quickly glanced at us, and walked out the door. Which made him even more intimidating.

During that week, our class had started to bond and unite, although there were several of our classmates who clearly didn't seem to fit the mold of the FBI. One, an attorney from North Carolina who had been a former deputy district attorney, resigned on Friday of our first week. No one knew why, but that morning Tom Jensen, our class counselor, met with us in the gym and announced the trainee was no longer with us. "One down and how many to go?" Jensen deadpanned.

Not a sound was heard. I suspect everyone was thinking the same thing I was: *Will the next one be me?*

Eleven

Another Dose of Reality

The "Boardroom" was its official name, but most everyone simply called it the "beer hall." Hoover's wisdom was again apparent in the addition of a bar within the academy buildings. When the academy was housed in the old Post Office building in Washington, D.C., one of Hoover's nightmares was that his agents would be out on the town, drinking, socializing and carousing with unsavory women, and even getting arrested by the local police for some drinking-related offense. A new agent incurring such legal problems would, of course, be immediately fired. Knowing his agents would drink, Hoover decided to prevent some problems by putting a drinking establishment within the walls of the FBI Academy. If he could control it to the extent they weren't out driving, that would save the bureau some embarrassing problems. The concept of *Don't Embarrass the Bureau* was the most important one to the Director. It was he who came up with the FBI motto "Fidelity, Bravery and Integrity," carved out of the initials of the bureau. The motto was present on the FBI seal and every other document or plaque associated with the bureau. Hoover was deadly serious about those three words.

Conveniently, the Boardroom was located right outside the doors of the cafeteria, so if one chose to do so, he or she could easily enjoy dinner, then enjoy the rest of the night drinking favorite adult beverages. Beer was the most popular, but a full range of hard drinks was also available.

Probably able to seat about one hundred and fifty people, it was a decently appointed place with plain tables and heavy plastic chairs. A limited menu was also available. Most nights the place was rocking by its 10:00 p.m. closing time.

Beginning at about seven o'clock every night, the beer hall began filling with National Academy students, agents attending in-service classes, and a smattering of new agents. On this particular Friday night, we were surrounded by a group of so-called *snake eaters*, the macho men of the FBI, a group of SWAT Team agents who were at the academy for a two-week in-service class. The testosterone level was as high as I'd ever seen it in one place, and I'd been around cops for nearly ten years. When a female would come through the door, one particular dark-haired, handsome SWAT agent would start the song, *"There she was just a-walking down the street, singin' do wah diddy diddy dum diddy dum...."* At which point the entire SWAT team choir would eagerly join in. Emboldened by a sufficient quantity of beer and the occasional hard drink, the agents would then plead with the woman to join them at the table. And, of course, none did. Which was a wise decision.

Seated at the table to my rear was an agent from the Los Angeles office, and we began a conversation that would prove to be somewhat instructive to my stress level at the academy.

"This place is a joke," he said. "It's bullshit, and it does absolutely nothing to get you ready for what you're going to face when you hit the street. You're lucky to have been a cop. They're sending agents out of here who have no clue about what they're going to have to deal with if they go to a bank robbery and have to shoot it out. We might as well be throwing rocks."

I learned he was a former Navy SEAL Team member during Vietnam, so there was no question he'd seen some combat time and knew what a firefight was all about. "We're dealing with some bad ass people out there, and they continue to arm us with nothing more than pea shooters. Most of us have to go out and buy our own weapons, or we're going to get our asses kicked every time we go out on a raid. They're too damn cheap to switch over to nines, and if we don't get 'em pretty soon, we're going to start losing agents left and right. The world has changed, but the FBI is stuck in the forties or fifties when it comes to weaponry.

"But you know what," he continued, "you're going to do fine here. Don't worry about it. Just look around the cafeteria when you go in for dinner. Look at some of the people in the other classes who are going to make it through. If they can make it, so can you." I'd told him my stress level the first few weeks had been pretty high, fearful of getting dismissed or not making it through some part of the training, and that several of my classmates and I had been to the beer hall every night during our first week getting sloshed.

"They wouldn't have brought you here if they didn't want to keep you," he said. "No doubt about it." He asked me where I'd finished in the national testing for that year, knowing all agents were ranked on an overall scale for the thousands taking the FBI entrance tests for a particular year.

"Forty-fourth," I said.

"Jesus Christ! You think they're gonna get rid of *you*? They've already got a ton of money invested in you."

"I don't know. I certainly don't want to flunk out or screw up somehow. We already had one guy who quit."

"What was his story?"

"We don't really know. He was a former prosecutor from somewhere in North Carolina, I think. Seemed like a pretty nice guy, but after a couple of days, he apparently decided it wasn't the right thing for him."

"Another damned lawyer." He slugged down a huge mouthful of beer. "The bureau loves lawyers and accountants. That's all Mr. Hoover would hire back in the day. But there is no way they will understand this job as quickly as you will, or I did because of the military. They have never had a lick of experience dealing with assholes on the street like we have. They're naïve enough that they'd dig into a pile of horseshit looking for a horse. By the time they analyze what's going on, it's too late in a crisis situation. It's paralysis by analysis."

I thought of my class. We had several lawyers and at least two accountants.

"Look, I've been in this outfit for four years now," he said. "The best agents in the bureau are the guys who had some military time and ex-cops like you. Period. Are there some women who are alright? Yeah, some. But most of 'em were cops somewhere. At least they have some concept of the assholes we have to deal with out there in the real world. It takes 'em a long time to figure out what we're doing, but it's the same with a lot of the guys who had no experience with real conflict in their lives. Worst thing that ever happened to a lot of 'em was getting bullied in the fourth grade."

Another woman wandered in the door and my new friend joined in on another chorus of "*There she was….*"

He refilled his glass with beer and turned back to me. "So, what do you think about all that?" He laughed. "Sheds a little different light on things for you, doesn't it?"

"Sure does." I was simply trying to be agreeable, because it was pretty shocking to hear from an experienced agent. "I guess I always had this image of the FBI…that the agents were all like supermen or James Bond or something. The thought never occurred to me that—"

I didn't get to finish my sentence. "I really hate to be the one who bursts the bubble for you," he interjected, "but this outfit still has some big issues after Hoover checked out years ago. The old bastard was a tyrant, and he ran the bureau with an iron hand. No questions asked. He was far from perfect. Some people still wonder about him and old Clyde Tolson."

"Who?"

"Clyde Tolson. You never heard of him?"

"Not that I recall."

"He was supposedly the number one Assistant Director to Hoover, basically the number two guy in the bureau. They were inseparable and Hoover didn't have any girlfriends, so more than a few people wondered if they weren't…you know."

"Got it."

"And of course that ain't all of it. I personally think one of Hoover's biggest mistakes happened back in the early seventies."

"What was that?"

"He convinced Congress he needed another thousand agents, and they approved millions of dollars in funding. So he and the palace guard at the bureau went to work trying to figure out what to do in order to get a thousand new agents hired and trained in a couple of years. Not an easy job, as you might imagine."

"That's a hell of a lot of people."

"Well, some idiot at the *puzzle palace* decided to start recruiting teachers, of all things. I don't know how they did it, or who came up with the idea, but somehow they got the word out to teachers in the country, and thousands applied."

"Okay, so what was wrong with that?"

"Nothing but problems. Think about it. What's the mentality of a cop and a teacher?"

"I suppose a cop is anything but naïve, very alert to problems he might be facing, but a teacher—I'm not really sure. I mean if you train 'em..." I paused. "I don't know."

"A teacher's mentality is to help people, because they think everybody's basically a good person inside. A cop realizes there are some serious assholes around who can't be 'helped.' So, in addition to lawyers and accountants who have little clue about what they'll face on the street, we get about a thousand more with a naïve approach to things. It ain't good, buddy. You'll find out when you get in the field."

"I see what you mean. I had a great friend in my town in California who was a teacher. We used to argue until we were blue in the face, and we never could agree on much."

"That's just one part of it. The other thing we've got in the field are the goofy Foreign Counter Intelligence types. These guys must read science fiction magazines or something, because their squads look like the bar scene out of *Star Wars* or something."

"No kidding."

"Oh yeah. Wait 'til you get to your first office. You won't believe it. Look, here's the deal. Back in the war days, Hoover formed what were called 'security' squads. In theory, their job was to conduct investigations into people in the country who might pose a threat. You know, people who were from countries we were at war with, Japan, Germany..."

"Okay, so what's the problem with that?"

"It's a big deal, actually. Hoover took agents who couldn't cut it on criminal squads and assigned them to security squads. So they were pretty much populated by agents who couldn't figure out criminal cases, and guess what that means?"

"They weren't exactly the best and the brightest in the bureau?"

"You got it. And the worst part is, the FCI guys fell into some espionage cases like the Rosenberg spy case during the war. That gave them a ton of publicity and the old man liked publicity. So he started promoting some of those people, and now we've got a bunch of SAC's and ASAC's in the field who couldn't work a criminal case if a bank robbery happened while they were cashing a paycheck. I'm not kidding you, some of these guys can't investigate their way out of their own shower, but they're in charge of major FBI field offices."

"So, if I'm hearing what you're saying, if you're in an office where the Special Agent in Charge is an FCI person, you'd be wise to find a way to get on an FCI squad."

"You got it. We're like that in Los Angeles. Our Assistant Special Agent in Charge has an FCI background. So you can guess what happens to the criminal squads like mine which is bank robbery and fugitives, and the other reactive crime squads."

"You probably aren't held in the highest esteem?"

"Exactly. A lot of the bosses are a bunch of limp dicks who don't get it, and they think we're nothing but a bunch of jack-booted thugs and goons. Knuckle draggers. But some of these characters have never worked a criminal case in their careers, so they have no idea what we're trying to do. And more than a few of 'em are former teachers, so that makes 'em doubly clueless. Plus, the other thing they know is they can climb straight to the top if they can nail a few agents on the way. Doesn't matter if they're good ones or bad ones, and there are a lot more of the former than the latter."

"Well, that certainly gives me something to think about," I said as I got up from the table. I thanked my new friend for his candor. I was more than a little bit stunned by what I heard, but very little shocked me at that point in my life. I'd endured my share of issues while on the police department in California. The boss could be a big problem for a group of officers or detectives, depending on his emphasis or if he was a micro-manager. I tried not to be one myself when I was a supervisor, because the last thing a cop or an agent needs is someone picking him apart for little mistakes. Except for writing reports, and there I was a perfectionist with myself and my officers.

At ten thirty the bar started closing. All of the guys in my class had plenty to drink by then, and we staggered back to my room. Someone brought in a half gallon of

Southern Comfort, and we continued to drink and talk until past midnight when the booze was gone.

“You won’t believe what one of those SWAT guys told me tonight,” I began.

Twelve

Firearms Training—Day One

It took a few weeks to figure it out, but every time we walked into the cafeteria at the FBI Academy, the trappings of a 'caste system' were abundantly apparent. But you had to be more than a casual visitor or observer to notice.

The FBI National Academy students were the most visible, clad in their bright red golf shirts and tan khaki pants. Typically they would sit in clumps, with only the occasional NA student sitting alone or talking with a group of new agents. Often, the NA students who sat alone and didn't seem to want to be bothered were those from foreign countries.

Most instructors and staff members, plus agents assigned to the Behavioral Science Unit, were readily identifiable by their sharply cut suits and ties. Even the female instructors, of which there were few, wore business suits, usually dark blue with a white blouse.

Agents from field offices who were attending in-service classes were the most casual group. They were apt to wear most any combination of slacks and shirts, whether polo shirts or something else casual. Never a tie.

The agents who were attending the Management Aptitude Training class (MAP) were identifiable by their dark slacks, dress shirts and ties, with no sports coat. It seemed to be the uniform of the MAP trainees, often called the 'Make a Prick' in-service, presumably at the direction of the Management Unit at the academy. They seemed to associate with no one, often sitting alone at a table, presumably mulling new and exciting ways to motivate the unmotivated agents they would supervise in the field. Or figuring ways to stab other supervisors in the back to climb the ladder. Agents in the field called them 'blue flamers' to recognize their intense desire to rocket their way to the highest positions possible in the FBI.

The most obvious group was the instructors from the Firearms Unit. All of them wore dark blue khaki pants, a maroon golf shirt with "FBI Academy Firearms Instructor" emblazoned over the left breast pocket, and a dark blue hat with tall white letters proclaiming "FBI" on the front. Most of them were quite macho in appearance, almost as if the bureau required a firearms instructor to have a dark mustache and muscular body.

For a firearms instructor in a field office, the highest honor he or she could attain was to become an instructor at the FBI Academy. It was an opportunity to have access to every gun imaginable, which all of them cherished, and an unlimited quantity of ammunition to shoot. It was hard to gain access to the firearms unit unless you were in love with guns, and the term 'firearms faggot' was probably borne out of this unit. They were gun nuts at the highest possible level, possibly even as high in esteem as the Marine Corps instructors with whom they regularly consorted. They were prone to spend many of their off duty hours in the beer hall, talking with their associates about nothing more than ammunition and guns. Or the shootouts they'd been in. Or heard about. Or wanted to be in. Most of the firearms instructors weren't among the intellectual groups at the academy, but there was nothing they didn't know about their favorite topic.

The firearms instructor assigned to our class was Sid Talbot, and he simply didn't fit the mold of the typical FBI firearms instructor. Sid was in his mid-forties, hardly muscular in build, with a bit of a paunch and sloped shoulders which reflected his age and lack of work with the weights. It was apparent from our first session with Sid that he could care less about any trappings of appearance. His cherubic face was slightly reddish in the cheeks, wrinkled at the sides and neck, with a bit of a double chin prominent under a full mouth and no mustache above the lips. Lightly graying, reddish hair protruded from under his blue hat. He seemed to be pretty laid back, thus a perfect match for our class. Sid was clearly not someone who took himself seriously. But it was also clear from Day One that he took his instructional duties *very* seriously.

On Tuesday of our second week at the academy, we finished lunch and changed into our range clothes, grey shirts and pants with an "FBI" hat, to meet Sid on the range. The entire class was seated under a covered set of bleachers, with one of many pistol ranges ahead of us. I was excited to start our firearms training, although a bit apprehensive about training with the shotgun, which struck terror into my heart for some reason.

My shooting scores during our monthly qualifications at the police department had always been in the middle to high 90s, so I didn't anticipate a problem with qualifying at the academy. However, the specter of shooting a shotgun was more than a little bit of a concern to me. We carried an Ithaca shotgun in our patrol cars, but I had rarely shot it on the range, and was fearful of the awesome firepower the weapon could produce. Why I had this phobia I had no clue. But I had it, and dreaded the day we'd begin working with the Remington 870.

"Good afternoon, ladies and gentlemen. My name is Sid Talbot, and my job will be to assure that each and every one of you qualifies with your firearm at the academy." He had a bit of a slow, southern drawl to his voice, which wasn't unusual for FBI firearms instructors. We'd later learn Sid grew up in a small town in west Texas not far from Lubbock, and had graduated from Texas Tech in the same class with Donnie Anderson, an All-American running back.

We were sitting in a tiered, raised grandstand with wooden planks for seats, under a weathered shelter, on a clear, fall afternoon. Huge grass berms framed each side of the pistol range in front of us. I gazed beyond the targets at the end of the range, enjoying the pleasant sight of leaves on tall, thin oak and elm trees changing colors almost before my very eyes.

"There are several things we're going to try to accomplish today," Sid continued. "I fully realize some of you in this class have never fired a gun, or maybe even had a gun in your hands. And frankly, that's pretty normal. I also realize some of you have been in law enforcement or the military, or both, and are gun nuts like most of us here in the firearms unit. So we literally have both ends of the spectrum." I knew which end I belonged in, although I was far from a gun nut. I carried a .41 magnum revolver on duty with the police department, and had learned to shoot it pretty well. I didn't expect those scores to change much; if anything, my scores should go higher with some decent instruction.

"The first thing I expect you to do when you come to this range is to think safety, safety, and more safety," Sid said. "I have no desire to have any of you get shot on the range, and we will be firing live ammunition which can kill you or injure you badly if you or one of your classmates isn't careful out here. The most important thing I can tell you, and I want you to listen to this carefully is, do not, I repeat, *do not do anything* on the range until you're told to do it." He put a heavy emphasis on 'anything.' "You will not move to another place until I tell you to do so. You will not load or reload your weapons until I tell you to do so. When you are told to do something, you will not turn toward me to listen, because when you turn your entire body, your weapon is going to be pointed toward the person standing beside you. And with a loaded weapon, that is extremely dangerous. Does everyone understand that?"

The class, as a whole, nodded our heads and replied, "Yes sir."

Sid went on to explain more safety issues and range practices, and then told a quick story about the silhouette targets we'd be using on the range. "You'll notice that our formerly black silhouette targets are now grey. As you may know, we do a daily firearms demonstration at the FBI Headquarters indoor range. About a year ago, a tour was going through and, after watching the demonstration on the range, one of them sent a letter to the Director, Judge Webster. The letter essentially said, 'Why are you training your agents to shoot black people? Your targets are black with white backgrounds.'

"Judge Webster immediately ordered the firearms unit to come up with another target so as not to further offend anyone. What Judge Webster didn't realize was that our agents and officers *were not* being trained to shoot black people. At night with backlighting, it doesn't matter if a person is black, white, or orange. Their silhouette is going to look black to the agent or officer shooting. So we're now using grey targets on a white background, and that ridiculous change caused the bureau to spend several million dollars." Sid raised his eyebrows, clearly indicating that the appointment of a former Federal Judge to the position of FBI Director was not a popular one within the bureau. "When Mr. Hoover was the Director," Sid continued, "I'll guarantee you, nothing like that would ever have happened."

Thirteen

Special Agent Don Bishop

Our afternoon on the pistol range turned out to be more enjoyable than exerting. It was clear to me that our range time would be a stress-reliever, for me at least. For others, it was clearly going to be a struggle. Willie Austin, among others, had never held a firearm in his hands, and many were going to need considerable work and intensive instruction to get their skills to the required level. Those of us who had carried firearms as police officers or in the military were going to have a much easier time.

Sid eventually placed the class into our positions at the seven-yard line, each with a box of .38 caliber ammunition. On his instructions, we loaded six rounds in our revolvers and carefully put them in our holsters. "On the whistle," he ordered, "draw your weapon and fire one round at the target and re-holster your weapon." A group of about ten more instructors from the firearms training unit had mysteriously appeared behind our class, obviously knowing it was our first day and that some close supervision would be required. I assumed it was standard practice for the first couple days on the range for all New Agent classes.

"Is the line ready?" Sid looked up and down the line. "The line is ready. One round in two seconds on the whistle." He paused a moment and blew the whistle. We all drew our weapons, and I put my single round right through the center of the target. A perfect shot. Then I re-holstered.

We continued the drill with eighteen rounds, and I had a nice pattern going.

Shooting one round at a time was pretty easy. An instructor, whose name I'd learn was Don Bishop, came up behind me and asked, "Are you a former cop?"

As Sid instructed us, I didn't turn to face him, and then answered, "Yes sir." He asked me where, and I told him I'd been a police officer in California for almost ten years.

"That's great. You're going to do fine here." Bishop stepped back, saying, "Nice pattern. I'm anxious to get you on the shotgun range." Which gave me a slight chill of anxiety. I was more than comfortable with the revolver, but in my mind the shotgun was something like a sixteen-inch cannon on a battleship.

"We need to get together at the Boardroom later," Bishop said. "You going to be there tonight?" I told him we'd been there virtually every night, so it'd be a surprise if we didn't make it that night. "I'll see you there." Bishop went back to his position, more carefully watching the people on my left and right than me.

After we'd completed our single and double shot training, Sid told us to get another box of ammunition and make up some new targets. "C'mon!" he shouted. "Let's move. We don't have all day." The class raced to a large box of ammunition sitting on a plank on the grandstand. And then raced to paste new targets on the facer boards, which were actually pre-cut pieces of cardboard. The sticky glue we used was painted on the used target, at which point we'd slap a new target on and haul it down range to place it in the frame. I was surprised the bureau was using the sloppy glue instead of staples, but I assumed it was a cost-saving measure with thousands of people using the targets every year. Or maybe it was how they'd done it since the 1930s.

Sid gave us a new set of instructions after we reassembled at our appointed places on the fifteen-yard line. "On the whistle, you're going to fire three rounds in six seconds. Three rounds. Any questions?" No one apparently had one, so he ordered, "With six rounds load and holster." Everyone did as he instructed.

"One thing you need to start working on is your speed," Sid said. "When you're in a firefight on the street, you need to learn how to load that weapon quickly. What I want you to do is draw your weapons and get into a proper shooting position. You're at the fifteen-yard line, and your accuracy will not be quite the same. Is the line ready?"

Suddenly, I heard a commotion and shouting down the line to my right. I turned my head, and three instructors rushed to one of our female agents, a former teacher, who turned her entire body to ask Sid, "How many rounds are we shooting?" When she turned, her loaded revolver was pointed directly at the agent on her left.

"God dammit!" Sid yelled. "That's exactly what I told you *not* to do a few minutes ago. If you need to ask me a question, raise your hand and an instructor will come to you." He was clearly flustered. "That's exactly how we got an agent shot here a few months ago. Someone turned and fired a round right into the person next to him. Pay attention, damn it!"

Despite the faux pas by one member of the class, it was a great day, and I knew our firearms training would be one of the most enjoyable parts of the academy.

When we finished, Don Bishop came up to me again. "Good job, P.J." He patted me on the shoulder. "You might have a shot at a 'possible' if you keep working at it."

"What's that, sir?" I asked.

"Don't call me 'sir,' P.J.," he said. "I'm not any better than you."

"Yes sir."

"A possible is a score of one hundred on the Tactical Revolver Course. We only have one agent do it out of about ten classes, but I think you have a chance. So keep up the good work. I'll see you at the beer hall one of these nights and we'll compare some notes about being in Southern California. I was in L.A. before I came here, so we probably know some common people."

"Will do. Thank you, Mister Bishop."

"Don't call me 'mister,' either."

"No, sir."

Fourteen

And the Nicknames Begin

The classroom was deathly silent. A mosquito would've sounded like a fully loaded B-52 bomber buzzing us at a hundred feet. The story had been long and intricate, involving a kidnapped baby whose tiny body had been found in or near Gary, Indiana. Our instructor, SSA Marvin Johnson, paused, looked out at the class with an eerily serious look, and said, "The baby…was dead."

He paused again, presumably for dramatic effect, stared straight ahead, and scanned the entire class again. He briefly looked downward and slowly repeated, "The baby… was dead." Once again he paused and looked around the room at a virtual sea of anxious, awaiting faces. "The baby needed…mother's milk." Another dramatic pause. "Mother's milk." End of story. He turned off the projector, gathered his notes, and began walking toward the door, thus ending our day's lecture on Field Operations and Communications (FOAC).

Jim Mason kicked me in the leg with the side of his foot. I gave him a quick glance out of the corner of my eye and hoped our departing instructor hadn't seen either action. All the time I was thinking, *this is the FBI Academy. Be serious, you dumb ass.* I looked at my roommate again, furrowing my eyebrows. He knew I was laughing so hard inside that I could soak a double-wrapped set of Drypers' diapers.

We were in the sixth week of New Agent Training, and most of us had started to feel pretty comfortable with the routine. Similarly, most of us had arrived at a point in our academy training where we 'got it.' Those of us who *knew* we were going to make it, barring some cataclysmic and unexpected event or tragedy, could readily distinguish between the good and bad instructors, not to mention everything else that was flawed about the supposed West Point of law enforcement training. I was quickly getting the clue that the notion of 'highly-trained FBI agents' was much more of a myth than a reality.

The old perception and stereotype that all FBI agents were created in 'cookie-cutter' fashion was long gone in most of our minds. While some of the instructors at the academy were clearly the best available, it was obvious some were there for *other* reasons.

The famed television image of Efrem Zimbalist, Jr. and *The FBI* of the 1960s was fading fast as the model for all former and future FBI Special Agents. Most of us could see he was clearly the exception, not the rule.

All of us in the class had come to the academy with bright eyes, bushy tails, excitement, and the highest of expectations. It *was* the FBI, the most feared and revered law enforcement organization in the world. For many of us it was an unexpected reality check. We quickly learned that some of the instructors in the academy were, to put it mildly, dreadful and questionably qualified. Some had probably been sent to teach since they couldn't do the work in the field. Others were qualified beyond question. And they were our teachers and leaders in our quest to be Special Agents of the Federal Bureau of Investigation, in the hallowed halls of this icon of law enforcement training.

Marvin Johnson was one of the latter. An affable, personable, and sturdily built black man in his early forties, Special Agent Johnson was probably the only person in the room who didn't know he was there as a 'token.' Or maybe he did. Johnson was the only black instructor at the academy. While we all loved him for his kind manner and extreme consideration of the students, the class he was assigned to teach was probably the most boring thing next to reviewing the elements of a chemical formula for an English major.

FOAC was deadly. The purpose of the class was to review the locations, duties, and communication processes between all fifty-nine FBI field offices. Roughly forty hours of learning the methods to send an 'Airtel,' a gift of J. Edgar Hoover from the '50s, teletypes, and supposedly the basic FD 302 report forms. We were never taught how to do the latter. All of this was about as exciting for FBI trainees as watching a field of grass growing. While it was important, and we needed to learn about it, staring at a form on an overhead projector all day, and learning how to fill in the blanks for different problems and crimes, was not quite as much fun as being eaten alive by a Komodo dragon. But probably close.

Jim Mason had a habit of staying up late at night, knowing he could catch a few Z's in Johnson's class. Which was fine, until his head snapped back and he emitted an Olympic-class snort one morning in the FOAC class. He nearly decapitated himself with the sudden backward thrust of his head. Even Johnson had to laugh. It woke up Mason, but did little to change his sleeping habits in class.

A prematurely balding, thirty-year-old former college athlete and ex-cop from the East Coast, Mason was one of the most well-liked members of our New Agent class. He was a delightful, completely unique, and uncomplicated character without a phony bone in his body, who would go on to become an outstanding agent and eventually a Supervisory Special Agent in a large Midwest field office. But his attention span in most classes was seriously lacking at times.

Our class was an interesting and diverse group. Several former teachers, a handful of ex-cops, seven lawyers, the occasional and obligatory accountant, and a mixture of others, including former military officers. The class also included eight women, several Hispanics, and three blacks. As a group, we were the antithesis of the 'cookie cutter' view of the typical FBI agent. Our field counselor had told us that 20 percent of us would be gone by the end of our sixteen weeks of New Agent Training. And we'd already lost a few. It was a scary thought for me, and continued to be quite stressful at times. Thus, we'd often deal with the stress by getting totally hammered at the academy beer hall after classes were done for the day. And on weekends. We were a very unique class, and we remain one of the few New Agents classes, if not the only one, which continues to hold five-year reunions.

One evening, during a stress-relieving foray to the beer hall, the first of many class nicknames was conferred. There would be others.

Jason Freeman, a clean-cut former private practice attorney from Illinois was, like about ten of us, half in the bag one night at the Boardroom. He was particularly enamored of a female agent from San Francisco, attending an in-service class, who was sitting at an adjoining table. Freeman was doing his best to get the attention of the blonde FBI goddess, but every effort he made was rebuffed. Clearly, the female agent wasn't interested. But Freeman wouldn't take no for an answer.

"She said she won't go out with anyone who doesn't wear boots," he said disconsolately.

"Boots!" I laughed. "What's up with that?" I finished my beer and poured another glass from one of the pitchers on the table.

"Yeah, I'm not kidding you." Freeman took another gulp of the golden elixir. "She said she likes guys in boots. I don't have any. I'm a dead duck. I don't have a chance with her." He was devastated.

Terry Crawford, an ex-cop from Miami, was laughing as hard as the rest of us. "Hey, Jason. I've got a pair of boots back in my dorm room."

"No kidding! Will they fit me?"

"Who the hell cares? Want me to go get 'em?"

"Hell yes," he slurred. "It's my last chance. I've gotta get a date with her. She's a serious fox."

Crawford bolted toward the door while we discussed Freeman's predicament.

"Freeman, you moron," Willie Austin said with a chuckle. "That bitch ain't going out with you. It don't matter if them boots are made of gold."

Willie, a hulking Native American from a reservation in northern New Mexico, was the only person of his race in the entire academy. He commanded attention if only by virtue of his enormous size, 6'5" and nearly 250 pounds. But his sense of humor, coupled with the fact that he was the New Mexico Golden Gloves heavyweight boxing champion as a young man (as I would discover later), also gave rise to a different measure of respect. Willie was not a guy we took lightly. His pleasing personality, ready laugh, and sense of humor made him a class favorite. When he talked, we paid attention. "Give it up Freeman," he said, laughing. "Throw in the towel. It ain't gonna happen." And the rest of us laughed along with him.

Momentarily, Terry Crawford returned to the table, concealing something in a bag behind his back. "Okay, Jason," he said. "Here's your stupid boots." He handed them to Freeman under the table and returned to his beer.

Freeman carefully examined the apparent solution to his crisis, a high-topped pair of black dress boots, neatly polished and clearly ready for action. "Crawford," he said somewhat incoherently, "I love you."

Crawford laughed. "Hey, don't go fruit on me here. It's just a pair of boots. Try 'em on and see if they'll work." He swallowed another drink from his plastic cup.

Freeman struggled and snorted several times as he tried to get the boots on. "They fit!" he said excitedly, pulling the boot tightly on his foot. "Okay, I'm going for it."

We watched intently as he reached back and touched the object of his ardor on the shoulder. Her long, blonde locks swayed to the side as she turned and looked back to face Freeman. A vision of true beauty. A goddess. A true princess of the FBI.

Freeman raised both feet skyward. "Look. BOOTS!" he exclaimed loudly, proudly displaying his newfound treasures, much like a weasel would when returning to his lair and showing off a newly killed mouse to his mate. Surely she would be impressed and would finally relent.

She stared at the boots, looked at Freeman, looked back at the boots, huffed, said absolutely nothing, and promptly turned back to her fellow agents at the table to resume a conversation about some important FBI issues probably related to their in-service class.

As we roared with laughter, Freeman gloomily turned back to us and began doing what he should have been doing in the first place. Drinking beer.

We staggered out of the academy tavern at closing time, a happy little group of drunks, with one frustrated, wannabe lothario bemoaning his fate. And wearing the items that would eventually give rise to his class nickname. "Boots" was born.

I told the group, "We need to console our boy. I've got a half gallon of Ol' Granddad in my room." Which everyone knew was total contraband. We laughed and drank in my room until midnight. When the bottle of whiskey was gone, everyone went to their rooms and to bed. And Jim Mason fell soundly asleep in class the next day. FOAC could put a cup of coffee to sleep. Drinking was our downfall and we'd do more. Much more.

Even though J. Edgar Hoover was long gone, having died long before our class gathered at the academy, his legend and the mystique of the FBI persisted. We were summarily told, in no uncertain terms, that we had to fit the image, and should never embarrass the bureau. We knew that, *in the old days*, Hoover would order New Agent trainees to be fired for such reasons as having sweaty palms or being partly bald. It was all about image to Hoover.

On one occasion, the Director ordered the class counselor to "fire that pinhead." Not knowing who the pinhead was, the counselor picked about five candidates and dismissed them all, lest he incur the wrath of the Director. And so it went for many years. Some people said that even though Hoover was long-since dead, "The old bastard is still running the bureau." After a week of training, I could clearly see that was true. Image was critical. The FBI was known as the premier law enforcement agency in the entire world. A good part of that, I'd later learn, was myth and mystique, propaganda left over from the Hoover days. Another part was the awesome intimidation factor the FBI employed in its investigations. And the last part of the equation was pure, unadulterated bullshit.

And there I was, sitting in class at the vaunted FBI Academy, about to laugh like a hyena when Mr. Johnson left the room.

Fifteen

Death by First Aid Training

By the end of our sixth week, I was starting to get more than a little concerned about my level of alcohol consumption. There were only a few nights during that time when we didn't pay a visit to the beer hall. If we didn't get sloshed, it was a good gathering place. And we even spent a little time there on weekends.

I knew the academy was going to be stressful, and had quickly figured out it would prove to be difficult in some way to everyone in my class. There were essentially four components to the training. First was the academic part. In one of Sam Batterson's sessions with the class, he'd told us, "You will take quite a few tests at the academy. What you need to understand is that a passing grade on all the tests but First Aid is eighty-five percent. Most of you are used to seventy percent as being a passing grade in college. At the FBI Academy, we strive for excellence, and simply knowing 'some' of the information is not good enough for us. In fact, we don't recognize the concept of 'good enough' here."

Eighty-five was a passing grade! That didn't leave a lot of margin for error. If I got an 84 on a test in college or graduate school, which would probably guarantee me a grade of B for the class. What's wrong with a B? My daughter was a bit of an overachiever and came home with a B on a paper one day in high school. Since she was upset about the grade, I told her, "Loni, if I'd come home with a B, do you know how long the party would have lasted?"

"And," Batterson continued, "If you fail two tests at the academy, you're gone." So, the academic part of the academy was going to put some stress on me. Not that I was stupid or academically challenged in any way. I'd just finished my second master's degree in Public Administration from the University of Southern California before going to the FBI Academy. But a grade of 84 was a 'failure?' C'mon.

Week four of our academy training was partly devoted to First Aid. Our instructor was 'Nurse Mary,' a former Marine Corps nurse who appeared to be a major dyke, had a Hoover-like bulldog face, with dark, short hair, trimmed into what could only be described as "butch style." She wore the traditional white nurse uniform, and was about as personable as a few badgers I'd encountered in the Colorado foothills. Nurse Mary was very stern, and didn't appear to be someone you wanted to make a funny comment to, or about, and let her hear it. She was the only nurse assigned to the FBI Academy, and seemed to take her job quite seriously.

Her lectures were relatively simple, straightforward, and extremely boring. Using transparencies, she'd project the symptoms of various problems we'd probably never encounter on the screen at the front of the classroom. And we'd busily write down every word, knowing we'd have to memorize each and every one. For example, if shock was the problem, she'd put up the laundry list of shock issues, including such things as clammy skin, listlessness, and so forth. And we'd busy ourselves taking notes as frantically as we could. I felt like I was acquiring carpal tunnel syndrome after she'd completed four hours of putting transparencies on the screen, reading each one, and going on to the next, giving us time to dutifully write everything down. Her instructional techniques left a lot to be desired, needless to say, and I wondered several times why she didn't give us a handout so we could simply follow along and study it later.

But no. Nurse Mary would drawl, "Naouww, we gonna talk about how to deal with …" and away we'd go taking notes furiously. It was, to that point, the worst class I'd ever taken in my life, and when the twenty hours of First Aid was done, I had a massive amount of notes written. And had at least twenty-five laundry lists of symptoms written down which I could not care less about.

Rote memorization with no practical application is probably the worst of all possible ways to learn something. I knew FBI agents weren't out on patrol and weren't first responders. Thus, I questioned the value of what we were supposedly learning, not to mention the method of delivery. Learning mouth-to-mouth resuscitation and treatment for excessive bleeding would have been useful. Learning a bunch of worthless laundry lists wasn't.

"Naouww." Nurse Mary was concluding her final lecture on a Thursday afternoon. "We will have a test on everything I covered tomorrow morning at eight o'clock. You will need to memorize and repeat each and every symptom I've given you. If you get less than seventy percent on this test, you have failed it and you will have to take it again. It is not an official test at this academy, but you need to pass it. I will see you in the morning." She looked sternly at the class, grabbed her notes and transparencies, stacked them neatly, made what appeared to be a sharp right face, and literally marched out the door. The class sat silent and stunned.

"Oh my God," Jim Mason whispered as soon as the door closed. "We've gotta know all that useless crap by tomorrow morning? I can't do it." The room buzzed with similar comments.

"I'm gonna skip running tonight," Doug Stevens announced to the class. "Why don't we get together in groups later and try to figure out how to get this stuff down pat?"

"I can't do it." Mason turned to me and said, "I'm heading to the beer hall to get drunk."

"We've got to do it," I responded, not completely sure how it would be accomplished. But it had to get done, and done that night.

Sixteen

There *Is* a Doctor in the House

My roommate was a former star college athlete, but certainly not the scholarly type. He'd gone to St. Bonaventure University on a basketball scholarship, and had eventually gone on to work as a Pennsylvania State police officer before coming in the bureau. Jim Mason wasn't stupid, but he'd never been challenged academically on his march to being an all-conference point guard for the Bonnies. I was a little worried about him, but was even more worried about a man we'd all come to know as "Big Bob."

Bob Wallace was a gentle giant and one of the nicest men I'd ever met. At 6'4" of solid muscle, Bob had enjoyed a twelve-year career in the National Football League as a linebacker with several teams, including the Oakland Raiders and Houston Oilers. He was an imposing figure, a physical specimen, and a fierce defender in the pros whom I'd watched many times on television. Since I was one of the bigger guys in class, I found myself matched up with Willie Austin and Big Bob several times in defensive tactics. Wrestling with Big Bob was about like wrestling with a rhino, and his body was still solid despite his advancing years. Bob was at the maximum age of thirty-five when he started, two years ahead of me, but light-years ahead in muscular development and strength. I was literally in awe of him and would hate to think about ever having him mad at me.

One night at dinner, Bob told me, "P.J., I'm really worried about passing this academy."

"How come, Bob? I think we're all a little worried." I'd really taken a liking to the agreeable, easy-going black man, whose pleasant and kind personality was much different than the vicious tackler I'd watched destroy Denver Bronco running backs for several years while playing for the hated Raiders.

"All you guys got a real education in college." He drawled a bit when he spoke. "You're smart, P.J. I went to college all right, but I didn't learn nothin'. I was there to play football. That's all. They didn't care about classes."

"But Bob, all you've got to do is pay attention in class and take notes. I figure if you study your notes, you'll be okay."

"I don't know, P.J. I just didn't get an education, and some guys like you had some psychology classes and stuff they're talking about. You understand it all and I don't. I've been going down to the library every night and reading them psychology books until about midnight."

I felt very sympathetic to his plight. "Look, I really think what they're talking about in class is what's going to help you pass the tests. Just take good notes and you'll be fine."

"P.J., I don't think you understand. When I was playing football in college, we didn't even have to go to class. I'd walk into the classroom on the first day and my books would be sittin' on a desk with my name on 'em. If I didn't feel like goin' to class, I just didn't show up. Our professors knew what to do, and they'd do the right thing for all the football players. If I had a paper for the class, someone else would write it for me. And that's the way it worked for most of the players. Not all, you understand. Some of 'em wanted to get an education. But I knew I was there to play football. That's all. I was an All-American linebacker and they didn't want me to flunk out. So I'd get an A or a B in the class and that would keep me eligible."

"Oh my God." I was somewhat shocked. "I'd heard about that, but I've never talked to anyone it happened to."

I'd played a year of club football at my small college in Colorado, but we were not on scholarship and it was nothing more than an unnecessary activity that I gave up after one season. My goal was to finish college, and I knew I didn't come close to being an athlete of Bob's capabilities. There wasn't the slightest danger of me ever being drafted by the NFL.

After dinner, several of us decided to work off some stress in a different way than usual—by getting in a two mile run. Hoover Road sat on the east side of the academy complex, perfectly framed by a thick collection of oak and elm trees on each side. With the continuing changes of fall coming upon us, the long and daunting asphalt road looked particularly inviting this night, even though I hated running. My tall, sturdy frame was not designed for jogging, and I think I felt the pain much more than most of my classmates. Eight of us began the run, and my roommate stayed with me, although his inclination was to race ahead, which he was more than capable of doing. Mason's body, at about five foot eleven and 170 pounds, was lean and sinewy, and compared to me he was built to run. I was built to be a plow horse rather than a thoroughbred, so running was a serious struggle for me.

Later, Mason and I decided to invite our quad mates and my friend Big Bob over to study in our room. "I've got an idea how to learn this stuff," I began. "When I was in the police academy in California, we had to learn some of these laundry lists of useless crap. One of my classmates came up with a system he called 'mnemonics.'"

"What the hell is that?" Mason squinted his eyes and made an odd face.

"Here's the deal. What we need to do is come up with an acronym that we can remember and associate it with a First Aid symptom."

"Damn, P.J." Big Bob looked perplexed. "That sounds like more of a problem than we already have."

"No, it really isn't. Work with me for a minute, Bob. Let's say I give you the word 'shock.' All we have to do is remember the first letter of the symptoms and figure out a way to associate that with 'shock.' Here's my notes. Let me show you what I mean. She said the symptoms of shock can include low blood pressure, confusion, clammy hands, weak pulse, rapid breathing, and chills. So, we take the first letter of those and form an acronym. Let's see, if we take out the key words, we have a B for blood pressure, a C for confusion, another C for clammy hands, a P for weak pulse, another B for rapid breathing, and another C for chills."

I looked over at Big Bob and Mason, both of whom looked confused. "Wait, don't give up on me, this is going to make it a hell of a lot easier. So, we now have BBCCCP for shock. Just think of it this way...Big Bob would be shocked to be in Russia."

"Russia!" Bob looked even more confused. "Where did you get Russia from?"

"Ever watch the Olympics? What do the Russian athletes have on the front of their shirts? CCCP."

"OH!" Mason shrieked. "I get it now."

"We can arrange the symptoms in any way we want. If we write 'em down in some order, she can't flunk us for that. As long as they're all there, who cares about the order they're in?"

Bob put out a huge paw for me to slap five. "P.J., you are the man. I think you just saved us."

"Well, I hope so, but we've got some work to do." It was about eight when we started studying. And it was something like working a crossword puzzle. We'd look at our notes, pick out key words, form an acronym, and then relate the acronym to the problem she'd given us.

By eleven, we'd come up with about twenty-five acronyms to remember each laundry list, and had drilled each other on them over and over. "We're not stopping until everyone has them down pat," I said. I'd clearly assumed some leadership over our small study group, and they deferred to my system with complete acceptance.

Finally, everyone had them down to a science. "I need a beer," Mason announced.

"The beer hall's closed," I replied.

"Screw the beer hall. I'm heading into town."

"Jim, do you think that's wise? We've got a test first thing in the morning."

"Nah, I'm good. I just need to work off a little stress." He put his notes on his desk in the room as the other four of us exchanged glances. Clearly, he wasn't making a wise decision, as drinking was going to accomplish nothing more than to have him forget everything we'd just learned.

I was sleeping when Mason returned, slammed into my bed on the way to the bathroom, and finally fell into his own bed. I checked the clock on my desk. It was three o'clock in the morning.

Mason was sound asleep and smelled like the Jim Beam distillery when I returned from breakfast at seven thirty. I shook his shoulders. "Jim! Get up. We've got to be in class in a half hour. You gonna get something to eat?"

"Nah," he mumbled. I looked at his eyes and they were bloodshot and watery.

"All right, I'm heading down to the classroom to look over my notes. You better get up in a few minutes."

At one minute before eight, Mason came stumbling into the classroom. He'd forgotten his notes and parked his alcohol-soaked body in his assigned seat.

"You all right?" I asked.

"Yeah," he tried to whisper, still halfway inebriated. His breath could start a tree on fire. "I'm good." I knew he was anything but.

As the clock ticked off the last minute, with the anxiety level as high as it could get in the classroom, Nurse Mary marched in the door with a huge pack of paper under her right arm.

"Naouww," she droned in that annoying southern accent, "I'm goingta pass out these tests and y'all got an hour to git 'em done."

I looked at my test. All twenty-five points were listed with a space below to list the symptom of each issue.

I quickly began going through each question, listing the acronyms first, then went back and began plugging in the word or sentence to fill in the remaining information. It was almost frantic getting each acronym listed, but I'd gotten a good night's sleep, and that helped make my thinking processes quite clear.

Seated next to me, Mason was struggling. Which was no surprise after a full night of drinking. I heard him whisper "POSDICORB" to himself as he looked at the first symptom. And I knew the correct acronym was "BACTELOD." But cheating on a test would get you canned from the academy, so there was nothing I could do. He whispered another incorrect acronym to himself and I kicked his foot. I tried to put my test in front of me in a way that he could see it, but he didn't get the clue, even though I kicked his foot again. He reeked of booze.

It was futile, and I felt helpless. I finished my exam in a half hour, re-checked it, and handed it in to Nurse Mary.

Waiting in the hall, I was talking to Doug Lightner, one of the quad mates I'd studied with the night before.

"Mason's going to flunk it," I said.

"Why?"

"Well, he came in smashed as a possum on the highway at three a.m., and he's got all the acronyms we came up with backwards. There's nothing we can do now. I just hope Big Bob's doing okay. I'm a little worried about him, too. But there's no hope for Jim."

At five that afternoon, after another dreadful lecture on Field Office Administration and Communications, Tom Jensen, our class counselor marched into the room. As usual, Jensen was resplendent in an expensive suit, laundered white shirt, and fifty-dollar tie.

"All right, listen up," Jensen said from the podium, looking at a piece of paper he held in front of his face. "You all passed the First Aid test, except for one brain surgeon. Mason." He looked directly at my roommate. "See me after class." The rest of us breathed a sigh of relief. I didn't care what I'd gotten on the test, as long as I'd passed it. I looked at my roommate, and he was clearly disconsolate.

Later that night, a group of the usual suspects met in the beer hall. Mason was there with us, slopping down huge quantities of beer. "I've got to re-take the damn test tomorrow. Can you help me go over the notes again?"

"Sure, Doctor Mason." And with that brief comment, we'd conferred a nickname which remains today. The guys raised their glasses in a toast. "To the Doc," I shouted, and Mason laughed right along with the rest of us.

Seventeen

Legal I

Our fifth week at the academy heralded the start of "Legal I," and Bill Stranahan would be our principal legal instructor for the twenty-hour block of instruction.

During the week, we'd have five separate blocks of four hours each afternoon. It was hard for me to imagine how Doc would survive this class, particularly after flunking the First Aid test. Little did I know the problem would be me, not our class 'physician.'

Stranahan could best be described as a certified piece of work. A huge man with the shoulders of a former football player, he was one of the most unlikely-looking attorneys I'd ever seen. Had I been expecting a three-piece suit and a serious countenance, I'd have been completely taken aback by Stranahan's appearance and sense of humor. His suit was wrinkled and loose-fitting on his broad frame, and his white shirt appeared to have been pulled right out of the dryer without being ironed. Even his dark blue tie was slightly stained with food. His sandy hair was barely trimmed and hung limply over his ears, with bushy and prominent sideburns. He was a good-looking man, with a square chiseled face and a constant smile.

"Good morning," he greeted us as he stood at the podium, turning on the projection system with its complicated array of switches and buttons. A slide appeared on the screen, the ever-present FBI Seal, with "Legal Instruction Unit, FBI Academy" in large, white letters below the seal.

"My job is to teach you what you need to know about the Federal Criminal Code. But first, I think it's important that you get yourself relaxed a little bit. This legal stuff is pretty straightforward. Maybe a little boring at times. So, I need to tell you a story of some sort at the start of each class session. It's my theory that if I start you out by laughing, I will then bond with you and you'll get to understand me and the topic a lot better." His delivery was deadpanned, and he gazed out at the class, which was completely silent.

"All right," he began. "This seventy-year-old man goes into the doctor's office for an appointment. He'd been there many times before, and he knew the receptionist was nosey and would ask him some questions about why he was there. Which she did, by merrily saying 'Good morning, sir. Why are you here to see the doctor this morning?' And the old man answered, 'I'm having a problem with my dick.'"

I looked over at Doc, who had already doubled over laughing, even before the punch line was to be delivered.

"'Sir, I'm sorry, but there are other people in this waiting room. Can you figure out another way to say what your problem is so it won't upset them?'" Stranahan continued. "'Yes ma'am.' The old man left the office and returned, approaching the desk and the receptionist a second time. 'Good morning, sir,' the receptionist greeted him again. 'Why do you need to see the doctor this morning?' 'I'm having a problem with my ear.' 'Very good sir.' The other people in the waiting room listened attentively. 'And what's the problem with your ear?' 'I can't piss out of it.'"

Doc nearly fell out of his chair. I immediately held up both hands, with all ten fingers raised. Several other classmates did the same, as if we were judges at a diving or ice skating event, giving our scores. But for the quality of the joke, not for the performance in the pool or on the ice.

Stranahan looked at my nametag. "Mr. Klein," he said, as the class continued to chuckle. "Are you somehow responsible for rating the quality of jokes in this classroom?"

"Yes sir," I responded. "You're our first 'perfect ten.'"

He laughed. "Well, Mister Klein, Thank you. I'm very appreciative of that. Very appreciative. I've never had my jokes 'rated' before in the academy, and I've taught here for two years. Does this class rate all the instructor's jokes, Mister Klein?"

"Yes sir. But most of 'em don't tell jokes."

"Is there a reason why you do that, Mister Klein?"

"Yes sir. This is a very interesting class."

"I think I'm starting to get that impression."

"Thank you, sir."

"Does anyone in this class drink, Mister Klein?"

"Only to excess, sir."

"I see, Mister Klein. I expect I'll see some of you later in the beer hall later, won't I?"

"Yes sir, that's very likely."

"Thank you, Mister Klein."

"You're welcome sir."

Stranahan had quickly succeeded in bonding with the class and did not appear to have taken umbrage at our newly-developed 'joke rating system.' And he was, in fact, our first perfect ten. Several other instructors had received ratings of 'five fingers,' which I decreed was the lowest rating possible. It was a very loose system, of course, and Nurse Mary was not part of the system. It didn't appear she knew any jokes.

His lecture was directed to the criminal process in the Federal Legal Code, from the time of arrest through the initial appearance for a defendant in court, and the steps between those events all the way through a trial in federal court. I took copious notes, because the process was slightly different from what I was used to in California.

He concluded the lecture. "Tomorrow, we're going to talk about the process of discovery and the various motions you will face before and during a trial. Are there any questions?"

I looked at the Doc and back at my tablet, thinking, *Please, please, don't ask any questions.* I had filled up eight pages of notes. My right wrist felt like it had been chewed off by a crocodile and I couldn't possibly write another word. Luckily, no one had any questions, and classes mercifully ended for the day.

Eighteen

First PT Test

Early the next morning we suffered through our first Physical Training test. Clad in dark blue shorts and grey t-shirts, all emblazoned with "FBI Academy," we gathered at the south end of Hoover Road. The serious runners jogged in place, while those of us only hoping to make it through the two-mile run in a time under sixteen minutes just waited and prayed. I'd heard that potassium was important to eat before running, so I swiped a banana from the cafeteria and ate it as we waited for Sam Batterson to blow the whistle. Several of the gym attendants were out to watch the class run, as if it was something of a spectacle. Little did I know what was coming.

At promptly 9:00 a.m., Batterson blew the whistle and off we went. I went into my normal pace, as Boots and the Doc, along with Derek Thompson, all sprinter-types, sped ahead of the pack. A few others with spindly legs and trim bodies were close behind the leaders. Willie Austin, Gary DeCamp, and a few of the bigger guys including me, laid back and conserved our energy.

Thompson had declared himself to be "Dark Clark" because his athletic skills prowess, in his estimation, was at the Superman level. In truth, he probably wasn't too far from right. At 5'9" and a solid 165 pounds, he was athletically gifted with speed and quickness, so it was going to be interesting to see how he'd do in a longer run. His speed and athleticism had already been noted by all of us in doing the short obstacle course in the gym. Our class surgeon, also blessed with considerable athletic ability, was timed in just over twenty seconds as he seemingly flew around the cones and other obstacles. While that was a noteworthy and impressive time, Dark blew him away by two seconds, easily the best in the class.

"Hey." Willie was already starting to breathe heavily at the quarter-mile marker. "It ain't about setting no world records. All we gotta do is be under sixteen minutes and we get maximum points."

I was puffing a little myself, always finding it hard to carry on a conversation while running. "Let's try to stay together and just sprint at the end. Let those rabbits run." The Doc, Boots, and Dark were already more than a hundred yards ahead of the pack.

The first leg was toward the north end of the long, paved asphalt road. The morning was fairly cool, so heat wasn't an issue. But I was sweating by the time we made the turn and headed back. As we ran south, approaching the steps that would eventually denote the finish line, several of the faster runners were already passing us going the other way. Which meant they were about a quarter mile ahead of us.

"Damn." Willie was still pacing me. "Those bastards are going to finish in ten minutes."

"Doesn't matter." I was struggling. "Just gotta make it in under sixteen. Let's keep it going. We've got a pretty good pace. We ought to make it fine."

At the end of the road, we made the turn at a metal gate and headed back north toward the finish line.

"You ready?" Willie puffed and stepped up the pace. "Let's go." I paced the huge Native American for about a hundred yards, and then he sprinted away from me. About ten or twelve of our classmates finished ahead of us and were standing near the finish line clapping and cheering. "C'mon Willie!" they shouted and clapped. "Let's go, P.J.!"

Tom Jensen was standing at the finish line with a stopwatch, as usual dressed stylishly in a suit. "Thirteen ten," he said as Willie crossed the line and stopped, placing his hands on his thighs, nearly collapsing.

"Come on P.J., step it up!" Doc screamed and clapped.

"Thirteen twenty." Jensen announced my time as our classmates clapped their approval. I joined Willie and started sweating profusely as we rested in the grassy area beside the pavement.

"We did it, bud." He put out an open hand and I slapped five with him.

Willie and I had finished in the middle of the pack, and several others started steaming in after we completed our run. Boots ran the best time, an amazing ten minutes and twelve seconds. Several of the women in the class were walking at the south end of Hoover Road, as was Chip Taylor, an accountant from Upper New York.

When I'd first seen Chip at the FBI Building in D.C., my thought was, *how in the hell did this guy get in the FBI*? His face was reddish and puffy, with prominent rolls of fat hanging from his jowls. At an inch under six feet tall, he easily weighed in at around 240 pounds, and it was anything but solid. His gut hung prominently over his belt, and he couldn't begin to button his suit coat. I didn't know how the Applicant Coordinator in his processing Field Office could possibly have justified sending someone in such poor shape to the FBI Academy.

Several of our classmates finished toward the back of the pack, some walking across the finish line at the twenty-minute mark. One of our women was limping badly and holding her leg. Nicole Jackson, who showed up at the academy in good shape, finished in the top ten, well ahead of Willie and me. Chip Taylor barely made it in twenty-four minutes, walking slowly to the line and finishing dead last. While we stood at the finish line, clapping and cheering for our classmates to finish their "run," several of us wondered how Chip and a few of the women in our class would ever conquer the sixteen-minute barrier. And we knew if they didn't, that would be the end of their training at the academy.

Nineteen

Stories in the Boardroom

The successful completion of our first Physical Training test seemed to provide an excellent opportunity for several of us to celebrate that night. Or perhaps it was simply another excuse to head to the beer hall for our favorite social activity. Not that we needed one. We'd only missed a few nights in the prior weeks.

Don Bishop, my favorite firearms instructor, was finishing his third or fourth bourbon and water when we arrived. He joined all ten of us at our table when I greeted him and beckoned him over.

"So, P.J." Don sat down, slurring his words slightly. "How'd the PT test go today?" He was a tall, thin man with a slender face and a long, pointed nose with wisps of hair coming out of the nostrils. I guessed his height at about 6'3", and his weight around 180 pounds. His demeanor was calm and kind, very much unlike what I'd expect from one of the macho men from the Firearms Training Unit.

"Well," I replied. "Not too bad really. I did the two-mile run in a little over thirteen minutes, but I really need to work on my upper body strength."

"How come?"

"I only did three of the required six pull-ups."

"Just get in the weight room and you can solve that pretty fast."

"Yeah, I suppose I need to do that, but getting out and running a couple times a week is about all the PT I feel like engaging in. I'm not one of those workout Nazis like our boy Flex."

"Who's that?" Don took a gulp of his drink.

"Tony Martinez. Do you know him?"

"Is he that Hispanic guy?"

"Yeah. The one who was a former Marine Corps officer."

"A bit of a loner isn't he?"

"Seems that way." Martinez was a body builder who spent an inordinate amount of time in the weight room. One day when several of us decided to hit the weights a little bit, we wandered into the weight room, and there was Martinez standing in front of the mirrors flexing his muscles. And so the nickname "Flex" stuck, although it wasn't something we shared with Tony.

"There's a few of them running around here," Don said.

"Yeah, I noticed that. During our first week, a couple of them suddenly appeared in the gym."

"Let's see. That would be Frank McCann and John Distephano."

"I'm not sure about the names, but as soon as our class got onto the mats, two guys went parading through in gym shorts, like peacocks showing off their bodies for all of the girls in the class. It was pretty obvious."

Don chuckled. "That's normal. Both of them think the women will fall all over them when they see how well built they are. Distephano is a piece of work. He's one of the instructors in the Communication Arts Unit. A few months ago he got a complaint from a mother and her daughter. It seems he'd met the mother at a bar in Quantico and started porking her. Not too long after that, he also started hosing the daughter, which would have been fine, except she was seventeen years old. Not a good thing."

"So what did they do?"

"Not sure. I think they pretty much smoothed it over with mom and the problem went away. The rumor was that

Distephano gave both of them a case of the clap and that's when the situation came to light. Ever heard the phrase 'Don't Embarrass the Bureau?'"

"Uh, yeah. Like every day."

"Well, Distephano got a few days off for dipping his wick in the wrong place."

"I understand how it can happen. When I was on the police department, we had a sergeant who was tapping a sixteen-year-old police cadet. It wound up in the papers and he was charged with stat rape by the D.A.'s office. About a month before the trial was going to start, he married the girl. So, that ruled her out as a witness."

"Happens everywhere, doesn't it?"

"Yeah, I suppose so, but I guess I didn't think stuff like that would happen in the bureau."

"How little you know, my son!"

"I'm sure I'll find out more."

"You wouldn't believe the stuff that happens," Don said. "A few months ago, there was a supervisor in Los Angeles arrested for getting a blow job from a hooker in his bureau car. A patrol officer caught him red-handed, so to speak. About a year before that, the SAC got in a wreck with his secretary in the car. Rumor had it that she was giving him a little head when he was driving down the freeway, drunk as a skunk after the office Christmas party. They didn't arrest him, but the bureau sent him to Omaha to finish off his career. Boys will be boys."

"Wow." I was incredulous. "I never woulda thought…" I shook my head.

"That's nothin'. With Webster as the Director of the FBI, I think things are going completely to hell. The old man would never have put up with that sorta crap. Hoover would fire an agent if a woman even made a complaint. We had an ASAC in San Francisco who was drilling an informant a while back. Hoover would've either shit canned him or sent him to Butte. Maybe Anchorage. No questions asked. Webster gives him a few days off and the guy winds up getting married to the gal. And she was a hooker to boot."

"Oh my God."

"True story. And there are hundreds of 'em. Don't think for a minute that anything that can happen to any other guy can't happen to an FBI agent. We have a guy in L.A. who somehow got to be a good friend of Hugh Hefner. So he hangs out at the Playboy Mansion all the time, and if you're a member of the "Palace Guard,' which is the in-crowd in L.A., you get to attend parties, too. Do you think that sorta thing would happen when Mr. Hoover was running this outfit? Hell no!"

"Sounds like Hoover woulda been hanging out there himself from what I hear," I said.

"Probably woulda been," Don replied. The old bastard was a tyrant, but he could run the hell out of the FBI. We were all scared shitless of him, but he kept us on the straight and narrow. Where do you think the phrase 'Don't Embarrass the Bureau' comes from? Hoover."

"I suppose it was a climate of fear, but that's not always a bad thing either."

"Fear hardly explains it. If he said jump, you didn't even stop to ask 'how high?' The old bastard was like God when he came to do an office inspection. And he loved to go out to L.A., because he could socialize with all the movie stars and bet the ponies at Hollywood Park. I was out there a few times when he came out. He'd do it about twice a year. Sometimes more. He was like a celebrity to those people. 'Mr. FBI.' And he played it up to the hilt. 'Mr. G-Man.' He was like a rock star. He squired around a couple women out there for appearances sake, most of us think, because I don't think there was much doubt that he was porking old Clyde Tolson."

"I heard a little about that."

"Yeah, I'm pretty sure it was true. Where you saw Hoover, you saw Clyde. They did everything but hold hands. Inseparable. Definitely a couple. It was as obvious as the nose on my face." He laughed. "But I'll tell you what. No one in the media was going to print anything about it, because Hoover would discredit them in a minute. He had something on every one of those bastards, and they knew it. If someone even thought about saying something untoward about him, all he had to do was threaten them with getting their file out of his office and releasing information about them being a homo or something. His credibility was much higher than anyone in the country. Even all the presidents he served under. They were scared shitless of him, and he could play the game unlike anyone this country has ever seen."

"Something tells me, from what little I've seen, that he's still running the FBI."

"You got that right. All of the old guys in the upper echelon are still Hooverites. They were as loyal as hell to him, and they can't help but run the bureau the way they learned from the old man. It's still a climate of fear. Nothing has changed, and it's going to take years until guys like you get into management positions and start making changes. I'll be long retired by then."

"Not me. I'm going to be very happy being an agent. It was what I wanted to do when I was sixteen, and it's all I want to do. I spent about six years supervising and managing people before I came in the FBI, and that was enough for me. I just wanna be the best agent I can be, put in a good twenty years or so, and that'll suit me just fine."

"I like that attitude. Even though they call us 'Supervisory Special Agents' back here, I'm anything but a supervisor. Well, I suppose when I'm teaching a class or I'm out on the range that puts me in charge of people. But all I want to do is teach my classes as well as I can and get out of this outfit."

"Works for me, too."

The waitress came by. Don ordered another drink and asked me, "What're you drinking?"

"Just beer."

He told the waitress, "Bring him a pitcher."

"Thanks, Don." All I needed was a full pitcher to be completely sloshed before I went to bed. Luckily the next day was Saturday.

When the drinks arrived, he continued. "I gotta tell you a story about Hoover. If this doesn't show you how scared everyone was of him, I don't know what does. Years ago, a custodian was cleaning out his office when he was out of town one afternoon for some meeting. Hoover had his personal bathroom attached to his office, and there was a glass he'd kept on the sink for years. I guess he used it to brush his teeth or something. Anyhow, the janitor bumps into the glass and it breaks. Okay, no big thing right?"

"Well, it would seem that way."

"But no. This glass had been in there for years and had a little crack in it. Everybody assumed the old man loved the glass, because he never complained about it or asked for another one. So, they were in a panic. His secretary called a couple of the Assistant Directors. It was a huge crisis. The whole damn FBI shut down. 'What're we going to do?'

"So, the ADs came up with an idea. They sent someone out to buy a case of the same type of glasses, and sent them down to the lab. Some of the guys down there were assigned to crack the glass in exactly the same way the old one had been cracked. How they knew that, I don't know, but somehow they had an idea of just how the old glass was cracked. And they just knew Hoover loved that old glass. Anyhow, they went through a couple cases of glasses, breaking the hell out of 'em. Just couldn't seem to get one right. The ADs were having a fit. Hoover was due back in the office in about an hour and they still hadn't gotten it right. One of the ADs finally decided to just take a new glass and put it in the bathroom. 'Maybe he won't even notice,' he told everyone else. About a half hour later, Hoover comes rolling into the office. A couple of ADs were there ready to panic when the shit hit the fan. Hoover went straight into the bathroom. A few minutes later they heard the toilet flush, and out he comes. He looks at them and says, 'Someone finally changed that old broken glass in my bathroom. It's about time.' He headed to his desk and went to work, and nothing else was ever said."

"Oh my God, does that little story speak volumes or what?"

"That's the way it was. The old man scared the hell outta everybody. He had some sort of a fetish about taking left turns too. Or at least everybody thought he did, because he once said something about a bureau car wreck being caused when an agent was making an illegal left turn. So when I was out in L.A. and he'd come to town, they came up with a route to the office from the airport which didn't include any left turns being made. You think that was easy? Not hardly. But they'd pick the old man up at the airport in this huge limo, and away the procession would go with not a left turn being made all the way to the office on Wilshire." All I could do was shake my head.

"And they had to do the same thing on the way back to the airport, plus to every place they'd take him. One day they were taking him to some fancy joint on Sunset Boulevard to meet some big star. The agent drove right past the place and Mr. Hoover starts yelling, 'It's there…turn here…there it is.' But the agent was afraid to turn because it would have meant turning left, so he went around the block with Hoover yelling at him. Apparently the agent said, 'I'm sorry Mr. Hoover. I didn't think you'd want me to make a left turn.' Hoover yelled, 'Where in the hell did you hear that?' And from that point forward, the drivers seemed to have permission to include left turns in their routes. But the SACs around the bureau were still scared to do it and told the drivers not to make a left turn if they could possibly avoid it, other than to turn left into a restaurant or something. Think that wasn't complicated?"

“That’s a great story.” I shook my head again. It appeared Don Bishop was destined to be a great resource to me for some of the more colorful events in bureau history.

Twenty

Jousting and Togas

Two identical, seven-story dormitories dominated the landscape of the FBI Academy in the 1980s. The Madison dorm was the furthest west and, with the Washington dorm, which mirrored Madison, connected to the cafeteria building and library. In the center of the four buildings was a grassy, park-like square with several stone monuments and permanent seats that no one ever used. The eye-friendly area was clearly placed there for appearances, to be admired by visitors to the academy. And surely was by the many visitors and dignitaries who came to the academy at various times.

In later years, National Academy students would occupy rooms in Madison, and the new agent trainees would be housed in the Washington dorm. During the time my class was at Quantico, National Academy students were interspersed on floors with the new agents. It wasn't always a good mix. It seemed Tom Jensen was rarely around, although he did have a suite at the end of the hall on our floor. Sometimes he was drunk and passed out in his room, so he didn't hear the commotions that often occurred in the hallways.

"Doc," I whispered, looking at the clock on my desk, which told me it was one in the morning. "Doc, hey wake up…*Doc!*"

"What?" He rolled over, barely able to open his eyes.

"Did you hear that?"

"Hear what?"

"I don't *know* what. Something in the hall. Something just slammed into the wall. Listen."

The sound of muffled laughter from the hallway was more than slightly apparent.

"Hell, I don't know what they're doing out there. It's probably some of the NA guys. I'd guess they've been out drinking or something." He rolled over and covered his head with the pillow.

I went back to bed, rolled around, wondering what all of the racket was about. And couldn't sleep.

While our entire class was housed on the fifth floor, some of the remaining rooms had been filled by National Academy students. Over the course of the five weeks we'd been at the academy, I'd met several NA students, all of whom were senior officers or administrators from various police departments throughout the country. Some NA students were from law enforcement agencies in foreign countries. Attendance at the NA was a highly sought after, prestigious, career-advancing move.

Doc emitted a snort, signaling his return to a state of slumber. I threw the covers off, rolled over on my back, and then got out of bed and moved toward the door, opening it as silently as I could. Looking to my right, at the end of the hallway, I saw something I could barely imagine could be true. Standing in a mop bucket with wheels, completely naked, was a man I knew, a police captain from a department in the western U.S., a mop handle protruding from under his arm. Positioned behind him was a sheriff from a small county in Kentucky. Also totally unclothed.

I put my head a little further out the door and looked to my left. A police chief from the northeast, similarly unclad, was standing in a second mop bucket with a nude undersheriff from Texas behind him. Other NA students were looking out their doors. It was a surreal scene, until I finally figured out what was happening: they were about to have a jousting match. *Holy hell,* I thought.

I closed my door and crawled back into bed, covering my head with a pillow. But it didn't help. In a matter of moments, I heard the rolling of wheels, spontaneous laughter, and a tremendous crash, all occurring almost simultaneously. And then more laughter. Then the rolling of wheels started all over again. I could only imagine what was happening.

The 'joust' between the officers was going to continue until one of the senior officers either met his demise, or was knocked out of his 'chariot.' A second crash emitted from the hallway, and then silence. I fell asleep at some point, wondering if anyone was seriously injured while jousting. And really didn't care.

While the goal of the academy administrators was to have new agent trainees intermix with and meet fellow officers from around the country, and the world, the differing agendas of the National Academy students and New Agent classes clearly didn't permit this assimilation to occur.

Most of the young FBI agents were afraid to approach the older, senior police officers. Similarly, most of the National Academy students looked upon the young agents as law enforcement neophytes and had no interest in associating with them. It was simply an unholy marriage born of good intentions, but a practical impossibility. While few new agents could approach the senior law enforcement officers from the NA classes, with over ten years in law enforcement I was one of the few who could with comfort. Many of my classmates were intimidated and avoided the older officers.

Incidents involving National Academy students were legendary at the academy. An NYPD officer once went home for a long weekend, returned to the academy, and was promptly arrested for his involvement in a drug-related homicide. Several of the more creative NA students succeeded in getting a motorcycle into an elevator and bringing it to the seventh floor of the Washington dorm late one night. Security was called after a number of wheelies were performed and the carpeting in the hallway was virtually destroyed. An investigation ensued, and several NA students were sent home.

The *coup de gras* was committed one evening when several NA students were drinking and playing poker in a dorm room. One student threw a match into a trashcan and started a fire that destroyed the room and left smoke damage in many others. The entire dorm was evacuated. Luckily, the academy was built of brick and concrete, or the fire certainly would have done much more damage. Alcohol was almost always a factor in the incidents involving NA students. Actually, alcohol was *always* a factor.

A favorite weekend hangout of NA students was a notorious meat market on the Occoquan River, known affectionately as "The Boat." Much like the beer hall, the nickname had stuck over the years and few remember its true name. Local women and some from the D.C. area would learn the beginning dates of the new National Academy class, and would flock to The Boat on the first Friday of the class's arrival. The marital status of the new students was rarely, if ever, an issue. The female population of the D.C. area was disproportionately tilted in favor of the male population, so it wasn't a particularly difficult thing for even the most shy of students to hook up with a woman for the duration of his training. More than a few divorces resulted from these hastily formed relationships.

One Saturday night, I was alone in my dorm room when I heard the unmistakable sounds of females giggling in the hallway.

"Shhh," a male voice commanded. "You guys aren't supposed to be up here. Keep quiet."

The clock said 11:00 p.m. and I decided it was time to get a good night's sleep. I tucked myself into bed and pulled an extra pillow over my head. Doc was still out on the town, so I had all the quiet I could possibly want in my room. Or so I thought.

I woke up at midnight, hearing a chorus of "Toga! Toga! Toga!" emitting from the hallway, followed by more giggling. More female voices and loud music. "Toga! Toga! Toga!" Giggle. Giggle. Giggle.

Nearly sound asleep and not wanting to get out of bed, I reluctantly got up, went to the door, and looked down the hall to discover the source of the offending noises.

"Hey, honey, you're sooooo cute," I heard a woman say as I stuck my head out the door. "Put on a sheet. C'mon… join the party, baby."

A tall, willowy, blonde with large, bouncing breasts and a huge hairdo walked toward my door, covered only in a sheet. I could see right through it, and it was obvious she had nothing on above her waist. She handed me the drink in her hand. "C'mon honey," she beckoned. "We need a few more guys. We're having a toga party and some of these guys are really lame," she whispered, pushing her way into my room, draping an arm around my shoulder, and rubbing her boobs against my back. "C'mon sweetie," she slurred.

"Nah," I said. "I've got to get some sleep. I…uh…we've got a test…" I stammered as she gave me a closer hug, turned, and snuggled her face against my chest.

"C'mon baby, puhleeze. You're sooo cute." Her words drunkenly ran together. "We won't hurt you."

"Yeah, I'm sure I'm cute, but I've got a test Monday morning and you guys need to keep it down." I pushed her out of the room and into the hall. "You guys better keep it to a low roar," I said angrily as I shoved her toward the party room. "Keep the damn noise down. You're going to have some serious problems if the academy duty agent comes up here."

While it was tempting to join the party, I was damn sure not going to get kicked out of the academy because of some drunk NA students or a quick dalliance with some bimbos.

This incident was somewhat irregular, but having women in the dorms wasn't unusual at all. Generally it was on the weekends, most often Friday and Saturday nights. These were prime times for the National Academy guys to head off to the notorious "Love Boat" on the Occoquan River. It apparently wasn't difficult to score once you were there. Since security at the academy was virtually nil, many women were smuggled in through one of the 'sneak in-sneak out' doors.

In theory, all guests were required to go through the impressive, well-appointed reception area at the front of the academy, sign the log, get a badge, and visit during certain hours only. In practice, some did, but more used one of two back doors to the academy, which remained unlocked until ten p.m. However, if one were to call a classmate, that person could easily come down and open the door. No alarms. And a night of fun could be had by all. Sunday afternoons, with many people off into town, was also a good time for some fun encounters in the dorms.

There were two different Sundays when I was heading down the hall on my floor, and heard the unmistakable sounds of sex being enjoyed inside a dorm room. I won't go into details, but it's probably not hard to imagine what this means. However, it was always in a National Academy student's room. A new agent trainee knew that type of activity was grounds for immediate dismissal. However, that didn't mean some male and female new agent classmates wouldn't visit one another on occasion. Because of our defensive tactics training on cushioned wrestling mats in the gymnasium, we referred to this phenomenon as "Love on the Mats." And that was often where it all started. When you have young men and women with hormones raging after weeks with no sexual activity, anything was liable to happen. And often it did.

Twenty-One

It's All About Marksmanship

"Ya know, Doc, I'm just starting to figure something out." I walked out of the shower and into our bedroom. "People seem to have some sort of a preconceived idea about FBI Agents. Some sort of a stereotype of what FBI Agents *are like*." I emphasized the latter two words. "It's like we're supposed to be made out of a cookie cutter or something. I've already heard it a couple of times, you know, at dinner from the National Academy guys or somewhere out there in town when someone asks me what I do. 'You don't *seem to be like one*' or even 'you don't *look like* an FBI Agent.' What the hell does that mean?" I'd been thinking about it since I woke up at six.

"I don't know," my roomie grumbled, trying to wake up. "Leave me alone. Shut the hell up. I'm still sleeping." It was 7:30 a.m., and we still had to have breakfast and get to class by eight.

"C'mon Doc," I said. "Get your ass outta bed. Let's get rollin'."

The Doc was never quick to arise in the morning. "I don't know P.J. C'mon…I don't know the answer to your stupid questions. Leave me alone. I need to get in the shower. Shut up for a while. I gotta huge hangover, dammit, and I need to take a shower."

"All right. Hurry up and I'll wait for you." I walked into the bathroom we shared with our quad-mates and splashed on some aftershave. Doc strolled in, turned on the faucet in the sink, and headed to the shower.

"Doc!" I yelled as he stepped into the shower. "Why in the hell did you leave the water in the sink running?"

"I always do." He closed the shower door. "It's a habit. I've always done it. I grew up where we had plenty of water. Shut the hell up."

I was aghast. "Doc, I grew up in the west, and I lived in two states where water was scarce and was at a premium. We always conserved. You're just wasting water. Why in the hell would you send perfectly good water down the drain?" I reached over and turned the faucet off in the sink.

"Cuz I grew up where there was plenty of it, you dumb shit." His voice sounded a little muffled. "Shut the hell up and let me take a shower. I don't feel good and I don't need any of your bullshit."

When we headed down to breakfast, I continued my previous line of commentary. "You know Doc, frankly, I never knew what it meant, but I always assumed people thought a Special Agent of the FBI was somehow supposed to fit the profile of Inspector Erskine on *The FBI* or something. It's like he was the icon...the bell cow or something. The role model for what an FBI agent was supposed to be like. You know what I mean? You've gotta be something of a tight ass. A real serious guy, or something like that. You know what I'm sayin'?"

Doc said, "Well, I know what you mean, but it's only taken me a few weeks here to get disabused of that idea. Some of the people back here are complete morons. I have a hard time believing the quality of people they recruited. There are some real yo-yos in our class and at the academy."

"I can't disagree with that, Doc," I replied. "But I think old Hoover would be turning over in his grave if he saw some of these characters."

J. Edgar Hoover died many years before I was hired by the FBI, but anyone who thought he wasn't still running the FBI had another thing coming. He created an air of mystique about the FBI that still persists. He dictated everything that would be seen on the popular show *The FBI*. His agents were deadly serious, maybe pricks at times, relentless in their pursuit of whomever they happened to be chasing that week on the show. And they always caught the bad guys and solved the cases. Without fail. There was an 'image' to maintain. A mystique about the FBI that Mr. Hoover wanted to continue ad infinitum. As long as he was the Director of the FBI, that's exactly what would happen. His agents were loathe to act in any way that would embarrass the bureau.

We completed our classes for the day, had dinner, went out for a two-mile run on Hoover Road, and were sitting on our beds when all of a sudden the door to our dorm room came flying open. The Doc and I were reading some cases Bill Stranahan wanted us to brief for the next legal class. I don't startle easily, but was so consumed with what we were doing that I sat straight up.

"Red handle raid! Red handle raid!" a cacophony of voices yelled as they burst into the room. Doug Stevens, a former accountant, was leading the pack, followed by two lawyers and a former teacher. "Click…click…click" was all I heard as I jumped off of my bed, ready to do battle with someone.

"Red handle raid! Red handle raid!"

In our second week at the academy we were issued what were called "red handle" firearms. The guns, all of which were .38 caliber revolvers, had been deactivated and the firing pins were removed. The handgrips were painted red, thus "red handles." There was no possibility that they could shoot a bullet, even if one was loaded. The firearms training unit wanted all of the new agents to work with the guns each night to make sure we had the strength to pull the trigger enough times to qualify on the range. Most of us didn't need to worry about it. Some of the females in the class did. Not to mention a few of the men. But we were reminded over and over that we should never point *any* type of a gun at another person, even if we knew it was unloaded or deactivated.

"What the hell are you guys doing?" I said, staring at everyone in the group of grinning new agents who had raced into our room.

"It's a raid!" Stevens yelled, pointing his gun at me and 'clicking' the trigger even more. "Red handle raid... red handle raid." He pointed a gun at me and continued pulling the trigger, laughing.

"Okay, Doug, the party's over." I looked at him and his cohorts with disdain. "We're tryin' to do some studying, so get the hell outta here before I take that gun and stick it up your ass."

If I sounded like I was pissed off, I was. I was close to punching out one or two of the 'raiders.' "Thanks for the raid," I said, and they were off to 'raid' another room.

I looked at Doc when the 'raiders' ran out and I slammed the door shut. "You know Doc, I would guess I was about eight or ten years old when my dad told me to never assume a weapon was unloaded. These guys must have never handled a gun before. Remember what we were talking about this morning when I said I had no clue how they hired some of these bozos? I rest my case."

"Some of those people may never make it on the range," Doc said. "I'd guess every one of those characters who just left have never had a gun in their hands before they got here. First time they put a gun in their hand, they probably popped a woodie." He looked at me, shook his head, and went back to reading one of the cases we were supposed to brief for the next legal class. "Bunch of damn goofballs. I just hope I don't wind up havin' to work with one of 'em on a bank robbery squad someday."

"Ya know, I think I've shot more rounds of ammo here than I did in all my years on the police department," Jim Nelson said the next night at dinner. "Firearms training is the only thing that keeps me sane around this place."

"You got that right," I replied as several of our classmates nodded in agreement. "We had to qualify every month, but that meant fifty rounds. And that was it. If we wanted to shoot more than that, we had to pay for the ammo. As luck would have it, I was one of the best shots on my department, so I didn't have to spend much time practicing. Seemed to come natural to me, I guess. But the problem was, we didn't do any combat or situation training or anything like that. It was all marksmanship. Aiming and shooting. Putting a bullet in the middle of a target. Bang, bang, bang. It was like sniper training or something. Our range master was great. He was a former military guy, but he'd never been a cop, so he had no clue about the situations we could get into. I feel lucky I only got in a few of 'em, and never had to shoot anyone. If my luck continues, that won't change." Luckily for me, it didn't.

Doc said, "You know, here's what really bugs me. This place is all about marksmanship. That's it. Period. End of statement. We aren't trained for any of the situations that we'll see when we get out on the street. When I went through the police academy, we had some of those 'Shoot, Don't Shoot' situations thrown at us. Sure, it was just in buildings at the academy and Motorola films, but our instructors made it realistic, and when I got out of the academy I felt like I at least understood some of the situations I might find myself involved in."

"No kidding," Gary DeCamp said. "It's like these guys don't care, or they just don't get it. That Hogan's Alley deal they put us through was completely useless. Shooting the long guns was about the same. Useless. Maybe something a Marine Corps sniper would need to learn. I mean, c'mon, shooting at a target from two hundred yards. What the hell did that prove? Sid is great as an instructor, but all we're doing out there is pasting targets with that nasty glue and cranking off more rounds. Don't get me wrong, I appreciate all of the ammo we're going through. But when I get outta here, I'll just be glad I've been in some of these situations on the street when I was a cop."

Nelson laughed. "Can you imagine some of the people in our class when they hit the street?" It was less a question than a rhetorical statement. "It could be ugly, you guys. Some of 'em have never been around a gun in their lives. In fact, if you look at the ones who are doing the remedial classes to qualify, it's the ones who never had experience in a cop's world. It's scary. I've been next to a couple of 'em on the range, and they'll just point their gun right at me without even thinking about it. And most of 'em are lucky to even hit the target, let alone get a score in the nineties."

"It's a damn good thing FBI agents don't get in as many shootouts as cops do in this country," DeCamp noted. "Every year we lose about a hundred and fifty officers, but in all the years the FBI has been around, we've only lost about twenty or thirty agents. Sure, that's not good, but it's nothing like cops face on the street every day."

I said, "The bureau has lost a few agents in the last couple of years. When I was in California, two agents were killed in one of the small offices out of the San Diego Division. Remember that?"

"I do," Doc answered. "They were in their office when some whack job came in with a gun and just started blasting away. I don't think there was much they could have done about it. The guy was some sort of a schizo I think. And if I remember right, an agent in one of the Midwest offices was killed a few days later."

"Yeah, I remember that," Gary said. "I think it was Cleveland. But how about the two agents who died on that Indian Reservation in South Dakota? They were just covering a lead looking for some guy when they got ambushed. I think it's getting worse rather than better."

"No kidding," I said. "My mom mentioned that when I went into the bureau. She grew up in the thirties when agents were shooting it out with all sorts of bad guys. Dillinger. Baby Face. All those characters. She was sure that's what I'd do every day. I don't think that's what's gonna happen, but I don't know. I just wish I felt a little better prepared than I probably will be when I leave this place."

"Really." Nelson laughed again. "And here we have these guys running around doing their 'red handle raids.' Scares the crap outta me."

Twenty-Two

More Death—by Fingerprint Training

I hadn't thought of torture much in my life, but on the occasions when I did, I always thought it would involve diabolical acts such as dripping water, strategically placed bamboo shoots, electrical wires, or even the occasional water board. Perhaps vices applied to body parts to create excruciating pain. At least, I *thought* these things would be involved.

Boy, was I wrong.

The worst week of the entire academy was devoted to a topic we needed to know *something* about, but not a complete week of struggling, if not *dying* to get through: classifying fingerprints.

And I thought First Aid was bad. That was only boot camp for this stuff.

Did we need to learn how to take a person's fingerprints? Absolutely. How to fill out the forms and send them to the FBI Lab? Definitely. How to take major case prints? No doubt about it. But we didn't learn any of that in our full week of learning about 'tented arches,' 'loops,' 'whorls,' and heaven knows what else.

At some point in the lesson, probably within the first two or three minutes, one of our instructors told us to go to a page in a manual they had provided each of us. And he read the following paragraph verbatim:

"The FBI recognizes eight different types of patterns: radial loop, ulnar loop, double loop, central pocket loop, plain arch, tented arch, plain whorl, and accidental. Whorls are usually circular or spiral in shape. Arches have a mound like contour, while tented arches have a spike like or steeple like appearance in the center. Loops have concentric hairpin or staple-shaped ridges and are described as 'radial' or 'ulnar' to denote their slopes; ulnar loops slope toward the little finger side of the hand, radial loops toward the thumb. Loops constitute about 65 percent of the total fingerprint patterns; whorls make up about 30 percent, and arches and tented arches together account for the other 5 percent. The most common pattern is the ulnar loop."

My first thought was, *this is going to be a very long week.* I looked to my right at the Doc, and he was sound asleep. And snoring softly.

Our instructor looked up from the text he'd been reading. "Do y'all have any questions about that?"

No one spoke a word, fearing he would drone on with more reading. And then he continued, "As I said, there is one more pattern, and we call that one 'accidental.' It's pretty rare, and we won't talk about that too much."

I was sure everyone in the class was, like me, staring ahead with blurred vision. *What in the hell is happening here?* I kicked Doc in the leg to wake him up. He snorted, glowered at me, and then went back to sleep. *Okay, you dumb ass. You're gonna get through this one all by your bad self.*

So while our fingerprint instructor was talking about "accidental" fingerprints, I was thinking, *this entire class is going to be* accidental, *if I pass it.* Both instructors looked like nerdy accountants, and their lectures were probably going to be about as interesting as an accounting class I took and dropped in college. But I couldn't figure out a way to drop this one. I could already imagine our final exam being an exercise in examining and classifying a ton of prints. Which I knew was something we'd never have to do in our careers as FBI agents, was a waste of time, an exercise in futility, and useless stupidity. And this was part of the reason they called us *highly trained federal agents*?

I looked at Doc out of the corner of my eye. His mouth was agape and his eyes appeared to be glazed over. It was only 8:10 in the morning.

By 1946, the FBI had processed one hundred million fingerprint cards in files that were manually maintained. By the late 1970s, that number had risen to well over two hundred million cards. Someone had to classify these things. None of those *someones* were Special Agents, unless they were specially trained examiners. A process which I was later to learn took several years. Not a week.

"Awright," the lead instructor droned in a Virginia accent that seemed to have some traces of Canadian inflection in there somewhere. He held up a fingerprint card. "Naouwww, this card is the same one that you see projected on the screen in front of you rat thar. See that?"

I looked up, and then over at Doc, whose head was nodding. He was clueless what was going on.

"It's also the first copy in the packet we provided each of you." I looked at the front copy, then up and back at the screen. *Seems the same*, I thought, and then I turned the page. *But it also looks like this one, and the next one, and....* This was going to be a bad situation for me. And probably worse for the Doc.

"Naouww, this is a classic example of a loop pattern. But if ya'll look carefully—" he used a pointer to outline part of the pattern on the board "—you'll see this is actually a double loop."

I looked. I didn't see it. I looked at Doc. He didn't see it either, because he was sound asleep. I just hoped he wouldn't snort.

"Do ya see that?" He looked out at the class. No one moved or said a thing. I was assuming some of my classmates were catching all of it.

"Awright, that's good." Our instructor assumed we understood, little knowing none of us had the slightest clue what he was talking about. "The next pattern you will see in your packet is one we call the plain whorl." Again, he looked up. "Do you see the difference?"

I didn't. Doc surely didn't. But our instructor looked at the class reaction and assumed we did understand.

The damn things all looked alike to me.

"I'll outline this one up here and you can see how it's different from the loop." He traced the pertinent area on the screen with his pointer. "Y'all see that?" I didn't. He presumed everyone had, and moved onto the next one.

"If you can get these figured out, then you will have over ninety percent of it done. So we're gonna work on that for the next two days at least." *I might die of boredom first.*

I kicked Doc in the leg and he snorted as his head snapped forward. He probably hadn't heard a word that was said all afternoon.

At dinner that night, several of us were talking about the class.

"Five days of this is going to kill me," Gary DeCamp growled.

"Why do we need to learn this crap?" Jim Nelson asked. "It's a damn waste of time. I mean, c'mon, don't they have something else to talk about that would be useful to us? We may take a ton of prints in our careers, but we'll never classify a set of prints unless we're stupid enough to go back to headquarters."

"There are a lot of people in this class who have never rolled a set of prints," I said. "They need to know how to do it, and they didn't teach us a thing about it. Not only that, they didn't cover a thing about how to take 'major case' prints. I'd like a refresher on that myself. But no, we learned something we'll never use."

"Hey look, I've got a way to solve almost all of our problems," Mike Toomey said. "Let's go out for a run and head to the beer hall." Toomey was a former police officer from Phoenix, a tall and handsome young guy with the characteristic dark mustache trimmed neatly over his mouth. "Everyone okay with that?" We all looked at one another, heads nodded in agreement, and that's exactly what we did.

"It might be the only way to survive the week," said Nicole Jackson, one of the female agents who seemed to enjoy hanging around with the former cops in the class. And we all headed for the gym to get dressed and head out to Hoover Road for a different type of torture than we had endured all day.

Twenty-Three

Another Night in the Boardroom

Since it was pretty late by the time we arrived at the beer hall, probably eight o'clock, we had some serious catching up to do. We'd gotten a later start than usual, and the place closed promptly at ten thirty. The group that gathered that night was comprised solely of former cops. To my recollection, it was the only time that had happened. Everyone else had gone to their rooms to study about loops and whorls. And to remain clueless about the mystery of classifying fingerprints.

I looked around the table. There were no lawyers, no teachers, no accountants or former military officers. Only cops. I think all the guys at the table realized it too, which seemed to create much more of an open atmosphere to talk than we'd ever had. Cops seem to understand cops and can talk to one another quite well. It turned out to be a long and interesting night.

Andy Krause spent five years as a patrol officer and detective with the police department in Brockton, Massachusetts. His experience in law enforcement was a virtual mirror of mine. He graduated with a degree in Criminal Justice from Framingham State College before he was hired as an officer with the police department, progressed into detectives, and then made sergeant before testing with and being hired by the FBI.

"I'm still waiting to learn something that's going to help me be an agent," Krause said. "This fingerprinting business typifies what a crock of shit this place is. My academy in Massachusetts was twenty weeks long and we barely talked about fingerprints. Anyone who has a drop of common sense knows fingerprints can help to solve a few cases. The bad guys know how to solve the problem—just wear gloves. None of us will ever have to do anything more than try to lift a print, so why don't they just give us some training on the best way to take prints, rather than trying to pretend we're supposed to be fingerprint experts? It's probably the stupidest thing we've had here, and there have been more than a few."

"We'll survive it," Gary said. "Just like we did First Aid. Just like everything else here. Well, everyone but the Doc." Our class physician, who was sitting to Andy's left, raised his mug of beer in acknowledgement.

"Screw you, bitch," Doc snorted, raising a finger at Gary with his empty hand.

We all had enough beer in us that laughter came easy and everyone at every table in the Boardroom looked back at us wondering what was so funny. But nothing was really that funny except our doctor was close to being hammered.

"You assholes can stay here and bitch about this place all night," Doc said. "I'm outta here."

"Where you going, Doc?" Gary asked.

"To the goddamned Tiki Fala," Doc slurred. "I'm going to stay up a little late tonight."

The Tiki Fala was a somewhat notorious bar just outside the Quantico Marine Base, where lonely wives and girlfriends of enlisted men and officers would gather nightly to dance and pick up men. The Doc had been there more than a few times, sometimes with his loyal companion Boots.

Jim Nelson said, "Doc, don't even think about driving. Those little Marine Corps cops like nothing more than snatching up someone from the academy."

"Yeah, yeah, yeah." Doc stood up and poured the last couple ounces of beer down his gullet. "I'll be fine. See you in the morning." He looked directly at me. "Wake me up." I nodded and he headed toward the door.

"Big mistake," I said and looked toward the others.

Nelson lifted his glass to his mouth and took a big gulp. "I just hope he doesn't get arrested. He's a great guy and he's going to be a great agent someday. Problem is, all he's got on his mind is booze and females. With all the saltpeter they put in our food here, he must have a testosterone level about three times higher than most of us. I haven't had a woodie in weeks."

Joe Mulligan, a former Seattle police officer said, "Well, woodie or no woodie, if the Doc gets grabbed by those marines, he's a done deal. They won't cut him a bit of slack. He's gone. They'll throw him in the can in a heartbeat."

"They've gotta catch him first," said Jim Nelson. "Doc's smarter than you think he is, Joe. He was a cop like the rest of us, and even if he's about shitfaced, he knows how to drive the car so they won't know he's hammered."

"Yeah, well, there's a million ways to grab a drunk driver," Mike Toomey said. Because of his last name, someone creative had given Mike the nickname of "Slipper." It stuck. "I was driving around one night minding my own business when I saw a car stopped at a traffic light. It turned green, and the car didn't move. I honked, but the car stayed exactly where it was. I'm thinking, something's wrong here. So I get out of my cruiser and walk up to the car. The guy is sound asleep. Snoring. I'm a rookie, so I wasn't sure what the hell to do. The car wasn't moving, so I wasn't sure if I could arrest him for drunk driving or not. I pulled around him into a parking lot and started thinking, 'What do I do now?' And finally, it came to me. I kept some firecrackers in my briefcase, so I figured this was a way to use 'em. I snuck up on his car and threw a firecracker under it. Next thing I knew, the guy woke up and took off down the street. So the report I did started with something like, 'I saw a vehicle westbound on McCracken

Avenue which was swerving back and forth in the traffic lanes.' Never said anything about him stopped at the intersection. The guy was swerving all over the place, so it was a slam dunk. He pled guilty and I never had to go to court."

Jim Nelson said, "Our chief had an absolute 'no tolerance' policy. If you smelled alcohol or saw some other sign that the person was driving under the influence, we booked 'em. No questions asked and the chief had our backs. I was driving around one night when I saw a car swerving back and forth. So I pulled it over. I walk up to the car, the driver's side window opens, and this huge cloud of smoke comes rolling out. The driver is a seventeen-year-old kid. All of a sudden, he decides to jump out and do some Judo on me. Totally loaded. I watched him flail his arms around like Bruce Lee or something. And then he dropped 'em…and started flapping all over again. Which gave me a good chance to nail him with a solid right cross to the jaw. It was a two-hitter. I hit him and he hit the ground. Done deal."

"So what happened?" I asked.

"Once I got him cuffed, I arrested the other two punks in the car for possession. They had a bag of grass they'd hidden under the front seat. The point to all this is, some of these idiots just make it so easy for us. I hope our class physician isn't one of 'em."

Twenty-Four

Worried About Legal II

The test for our Legal II block was reputed to be one of the hardest in the academy. And so I announced, as I stepped out of the bathroom toweling off, "Doc, I'm worried."

"About what?" Doc, who didn't seem to worry about much, didn't look up from tying his shoelaces.

"The test tomorrow, you know, Legal Two."

"Aww, c'mon P.J., shut up. We're going to study like hell and you'll probably ace it like you've aced everything else."

"Well, thanks for the vote of confidence and encouragement Doc, but if you remember I didn't exactly ace Legal One. In fact, I got an eighty-five on it."

"The hell you did."

"Oh yeah, I did. I got one essay question about charging people with federal crimes confused with the California legal system. So I completely blew fifteen points. Bang. An eighty-five. Scared the hell outta me."

"You didn't tell me that, you bonehead."

"I know. I was too embarrassed."

Doc laughed, finally looking up. "P.J., you're not thinking straight. There are a whole lot of people in this class they'd rather boot than you. You get along with almost everyone, and that matters, too. You shoot the lights out on the range and you did fine on the physical stuff. You're golden. They're not going to can you."

"Well, thanks Doc, but let's do some serious studying tonight. No beer hall."

There was some pressure on everyone at the FBI Academy, and the academic part seemed to be the one for me. The physical training was a breeze, as were defensive tactics. Firearms training was more enjoyable than stressful. I was one of the best shots in the class. But the academic part was different. My problem with the legal classes was trying to separate federal legal procedure from what I'd learned and dealt with in California for about ten years. The two were decidedly different.

"Hey, don't worry about it," Doc said. "Somehow we'll get copies of those old legal tests from the class ahead of us. We'll go over 'em and we'll be fine. If we miss a couple of questions, so what? It ain't about being first in the class. It's about getting through this damn program and getting to our first office."

"Yeah," I replied. "You might remember that night when we studied like hell and you still flunked that stupid First Aid test."

"Thanks for reminding me." He chuckled. "That was a little different than this stuff. The test really didn't count, and you'll remember I went out drinking the night before. Hey, don't worry about this one, P.J. We'll get the tests and we'll be fine."

Doc and I both knew that, in some mysterious manner, copies of tests from the legal classes, and other difficult classes, managed to find their way from one class to another. It was common knowledge, and even some of the instructors made jokes about the practice, looking the other way. The copies of tests inexplicably went from one New Agents class to another as each progressed from one week to the next. There was no question it helped, but the objective multiple choice and true/false questions were only a part of the problem. Legal instructors liked to play law school professor and give us some complex fact patterns, then have us provide an analysis to see if we *really* got it. That was what happened to me on Legal I, and I didn't want it to happen again.

* * *

We met a couple of our classmates on the way down to breakfast.

"Hey, it's the Bobsey twins." Slipper Toomey greeted us as we joined the line of new agents, National Academy students, and agents attending in-service classes. "Did you guys hit the beer hall last night?" he asked.

"Nah," Doc answered. "I stayed here and P.J. was in bed by ten p.m., snoring as usual." He laughed. "P.J.'s worried about the Legal Two test tomorrow." He looked back at me, and I rolled my eyes as if to say *screw you, Doc.*

Slipper said, "You know, I'm somewhat inclined to agree with P.J. This whole thing about losing our principal legal instructor and getting the new guy is more than a little troubling. I like Jim Hale just fine, but I'll admit I enjoyed Stranahan a hell of a lot more. Hale's a better teacher, but Stranahan was a lot more fun in class, and everyone respected him I think. Too bad he got canned."

"I've gotta agree with that," Willie Austin said. "All of a sudden, everything in our legal classes changed when Hale showed up. Don't get me wrong, I don't have anything against him other than he's not Stranahan. He just seems to have a little different attitude and emphasis than Stranahan did. Hale is a bit of a tight ass, you know, a little too 'lawyerish' to suit me. Maybe just a little too stiff and formal. I suppose he'll be fine, but the change of instructors has me a little concerned."

Several weeks later, we found out what had happened to Stranahan. He'd been cleaning his gun in his office one afternoon when he had one of the notorious accidental discharges. "I didn't know it was loaded," he told the Academy Director, but that wasn't much of an excuse. The ages-old rule was and always will be, "Assume every gun *is* loaded." The bullet hole in his door was a clue that it was, in fact, loaded and ready to fire. Next thing we knew, he was gone, and we had no clue where they'd sent him. His office was cleaned out and there was no sign of him in the building. We never saw nor heard from him again, which was too bad as he was the best instructor, and the least serious, we had. Even better, he would occasionally join us for a few beers and really let his hair down.

Twenty-Five

Passing the Tests Around

"Hey Doc, P.J. Look here!" Dark Clark and Slipper Toomey busted through our door just after dinner, waving some papers in their hands. Dark was beaming. "It's the test questions, baby. Let's get to work."

"I love you, Dark!" Doc shouted, reaching for a copy of one of the tests Dark was waving around. "Will you marry me?"

"Shut up you pervert," I said. "You're a sick tuna, Doc. Let's take a look at these babies, and then I'll perform the wedding ceremony."

"All right then," Dark whispered. "I love you too, Doc, but let's get our asses to work here, baby."

We started tearing through the pages, and then approached it in a more methodical way. Some of the questions were repetitive, but it didn't matter. The more we reviewed the more comfortable we felt.

"This is great stuff," Slipper said. "I have no clue where these came from, but I don't really care. It's going to help us pass this test and that's all that matters."

We grilled one another over and over until about nine o'clock.

"We've got this stuff down pat," Doc said. "I'm heading down to the beer hall. How about you?" He looked at us individually.

"Hell, yes. We're gonna ace this bad boy." Slipper was already headed for the door.

At closing time, we snuck two full pitchers back to our room and were totally hammered when we finally got to bed at about midnight.

After dinner the next night, most of the regulars landed in the beer hall. As usual, it was a celebratory occasion. "No doubt in my mind I aced it," Doc announced.

Jim Nelson said, "Well, I'm not sure if I aced it, but I know I passed the damn thing with a score better than eighty-five. That's all I care about at this point."

Seated to my left was Ed Mireles, a new agent from the class behind us. I'd gotten to know Ed in the early weeks of our training, and we'd become pretty good friends. "Hey Eddie," I said, handing him a packet of the tests. "Got a little present for you, buddy. Pass these around to your guys. Legal Two would have been a real bitch without these. Spread 'em around to your class and make sure to go over the questions more than once. You'll be good to go."

"Thanks P.J., I really appreciate it," Ed said, scanning through the copies. "You're a great buddy. We need all the help we can get."

There was no way for either of us to know that several years later, Mireles would be involved in one of the most famous incidents in the history of the FBI. We also could not have known how the lack of street survival training at the academy significantly contributed to the deaths of two agents and the wounding of several others. Including Ed.

I lost contact with Mireles for several years after we graduated from the academy. I was assigned to Los Angeles after completing the academy, and he went off to Miami.

One afternoon several years later, my mother called my office. Which never happened. She sounded concerned, if not frantic. “P.J., are you okay?”

“Well, yeah Mom. Why wouldn’t I be?” I knew my mom was a worrier by nature, but I suspected something was up since she’d never called me at work before.

“Did you hear the news?”

“Uhh…no, I guess not. What’s happening?”

“You’re not in Miami, are you?”

“Mom, why in the world would I be in Miami? I’m here. I’m just sitting in the office trying to get some reports done. What’s going on? You sound like you’re flustered about something.” Mom was known to panic at times, and I don’t think she ever quite believed or understood what was happening with me during my career in law enforcement or even during the Vietnam War. In letters, I’d told her we were headed to the Tonkin Gulf or, as we called it, the “Tonkin Gulf Yacht Club.” We had some dangerous assignments thrown our way, but I think mom believed my submarine was always just sitting at the docks of the submarine base in San Diego and I was kidding her about my trips to Vietnam.

“I’m sorry, honey,” she said. “I just needed to check. You know how I am. I was watching the news and I saw a story about two FBI agents getting killed in Miami today. I just wanted to make sure you weren’t down there for some reason.”

“Oh my God. Uhh, no Mom, I’m fine, but are you sure you heard the story right?” Many people, if they heard any three capitalized initials put together, whether ATF or FBI, they immediately assumed it had to be the FBI. Just like I did when I was a youngster and decided I wanted to be in the FBI.

“Yes, honey, it’s all over the news. They were trying to find some bank robbers and they got in a big shootout. Some agents got shot and at least two of ‘em were killed. I don’t know all the details, but I just wanted to make sure you were all right." Her voice began cracking. "You know I didn't like it when you went in the FBI." She also didn't like it when I went into the submarine service, or when I was hired as a police officer. Moms can never stop being moms, and I always tried to understand that.

"Mom, I'm fine," I said. "I'm just doing some paperwork and going home. But thanks for checking on me. I know you worry. I love you, Mom."

"I love you too, honey. I just wish you had a different job."

"Thanks, Mom. I actually like this one pretty well."

Twenty-Six

The Controversial Miami Shootout

I was stationed in a small resident office in the Midwest at the time my mom called, so as soon as I hung up the phone I called my headquarters office. "Have you guys heard about a big shootout down in Miami?"

"Yes," the female receptionist said. "We've been getting a ton of calls. Haven't you heard about it?"

"Not a word. My mother just called and said she heard it on the news in Denver. What's the official version at this point?"

"Two agents are confirmed dead and another five or so are wounded."

This was well before the days of CNN and MSNBC, so I didn't have the slightest idea if I would be able to find out what happened until the late afternoon news. But I was not inclined to be so patient, since an old friend might be one of the agents killed or wounded. Since we didn't have a television set in my office, I decided to head home and see what I could find on the local news.

A neighbor of mine was the evening news anchor with our local ABC affiliate. I called him at the station. "Bruce, what've you heard about a couple agents getting killed in Miami?"

"P.J., you're kidding. I thought the FBI knew everything immediately."

"That's only a rumor, buddy. We're like mushrooms out here in this little office. They keep us in the dark and feed us bullshit. Tell me what you know. I just heard about it."

"We're covering it in a minute. Switch your TV on and you'll get all we know."

"Thanks, Bruce."

I headed down to the family room and hurriedly turned on the TV. Peter Jennings' face appeared after an announcer said, "This is an ABC News Special Report."

Video of the scene began to roll as Jennings reported, "Two FBI agents were killed, and at least five more were seriously wounded in Miami today, during a confrontation with two heavily-armed bank robbery suspects. Several agents from the Miami office are reported to be in critical condition at local hospitals." Cameras showed live shots of the Miami FBI Office, and then switched inside to a press conference that was just beginning.

"We're going to switch our coverage over to the FBI office in Miami," Jennings continued. "The Special Agent in Charge of the FBI office in Miami has a statement. All right, let's go to that now."

A dark-stained, well-lighted wooden podium displaying an FBI emblem with a tall, handsome, well-dressed man standing behind it appeared on the screen. "I have a brief statement and then I'll take questions," he said. "At nine forty-five this morning, agents of the FBI office in Miami and officers of the Metro-Dade Police Department were conducting a mobile surveillance, attempting to locate and identify two men who had committed a number of violent, military-style bank and armored car robberies in and around the Miami area. Agents located a vehicle matching the description of one that had been used in several of the robberies, and an attempt was made to stop the vehicle. Two men emerged from the suspect vehicle and began firing their weapons. In the ensuing gun battle, two FBI agents and the two suspected bank robbers were killed. I'm not at liberty at this point to reveal the identities of the agents or suspects. In addition to the agents killed, five agents were wounded and are presently in the hospital receiving treatment. While the injuries are serious, all of the agents are expected to survive at this time."

The Special Agent in Charge, flanked by a phalanx of other well-dressed and official-appearing men, took questions from the press, and basically provided no further information. The standard comment seemed to be, "I can't comment on that right now since it's under investigation at this time."

I watched in shock, then grabbed the phone to place a call the FBI office in Miami. I knew they'd be buried with inquiries, but I also wanted to know if my old friend was injured.

"FBI Miami," a pleasant female voice answered. "Can you hold please?" The line went dead with some innocuous music playing in the background. And I waited. And waited. Eventually, the woman's voice returned. "Can I help you?"

"I'd like to speak to Special Agent Ed Mireles."

"Uhhh…sir, who is calling please?"

"This is Special Agent P.J. Klein. Ed and I are old friends. I just need to see if he's all right."

"Sir, let me put you through to our SAC's office."

"Hello," a male voice answered.

"Yes, sir." I'm sure my voice was cracking. "This is Special Agent P.J. Klein and I'm a good friend of Ed Mireles. I'm calling to see if he's okay. I just heard about the situation you've got going on down there."

The man said, "Mr. Klein, I'm the Special Clerk here in the SAC's office. He's gone now and we're getting a ton of calls, as you can imagine."

"I appreciate that, and I'm really sorry about what's happened. I'm an agent too. I'm just trying to find out if Ed's okay or what's going on."

"Sir, we've got a lot of agents injured and at least two killed. I know Agent Mireles was involved in the incident, but I don't know how he's doing right now."

"You're not telling me Ed's one of the agents who got killed are you?"

"No, sir, I'm not saying that. I know he was injured, but I don't know how he's doing right now. I'm afraid it's a little crazy here, so I'll have to ask you to call back later. We'll have more information then. Things are still a little confusing now. I don't know if any single person has all the information, but we're doing our best to get it all together. It's just going to take some time, I'm afraid."

"Okay, no problem. I understand. I can imagine you've got more on your plate than you can handle. I'll just see what I can find out later. Thank you very much for your help, and again, I'm sorry for what's happened."

I was at a complete loss to figure out who to call or what to do. It wasn't every day that two FBI agents died in a shooting and a number of others were seriously injured. I decided to watch the evening news and see what I could learn from that. ABC News reported, "Two heavily-armed suspects, William Mattix, age 34, and Michael Platt, age 32, were killed after they shot and killed FBI Special Agents Ben Grogan, age 53, and Gerald Dove, age 30. Several other FBI agents were shot by the suspects and are in serious condition at area hospitals." Even though that was exactly what I'd heard before on the news, it seemed to make me even more frantic to find out what was happening.

The only solution I could find was to begin calling hospitals in Miami to see if Ed Mireles had been admitted as a patient. I represented myself as Ed's brother, trying to find out what his condition was.

And it worked.

"Ed!" I was practically frantic. "Are you okay?"

"P.J.?" he said. "Is that you?"

"Of course it is. Are you okay?"

"Not sure." He sounded groggy, his words were running together, and I knew he must have had some serious painkillers in his body.

"Can you talk?" I asked.

"Not sure about that either. Lossa drugs and suff. You know. Maybe for a little while."

"Okay, buddy, I understand. I just wanted to check and see if you're okay."

"Well…" He paused. "I'm not sure yet. I've got some bullet junk in my arm and my shoulder. I don't think I'm going tits up, but it's gonna take a little while before I'm outta here. How're you doin' brotha?"

"You bonehead," I replied. "I'm fine. I can't believe you just asked me that. You are such an asshole. You're the one who was in the frickin' shootout. Not me. I'm just checkin' on you."

"Well, my mom's sure I'm a goner. But you know what moms are like. You still got one right?"

"Oh, hell yeah. That's how I found out about this. My mom was watching TV and called me at the office. She was sure I was down there in the middle of it."

"I get that." He laughed, but not nearly as heartily as I knew he was capable of doing.

"Are you gonna be okay, old buddy?"

"I think so, P.J. I got a couple of rounds in me, but they think I'm gonna be okay. I'm hooked up to all sorts of stuff here. I'm thinking it's like the old days at the academy when you had us hooked up to those intravenous lines of booze."

I laughed. "Ed, you are the craziest person I know and getting worse. I'm trying to find out if you're okay and you're being an asshole as usual. I'll assume you're gonna be all right if you're cracking jokes."

"Hey, bud. I'm gonna be fine. Check back with me. I'm sorta fadin' out on you, and I've got some cute little nurse here wanting to do something to me."

"I don't even want to know what that 'something' is. Let me talk to her for a second."

"All right. Hey P.J., thanks for checkin' on me, my brotha."

"I love you, buddy."

"Love you too. Here's my nurse."

A female voice with a distinct Spanish accent said what sounded like "Jello?"

I hoped she could understand me. I talked as slowly as possible. "Yes, ma'am. I just wanted to let you know that your patient is most dangerous when he's in a horizontal position."

She seemed to understand, laughed, and handed the phone back to Ed.

"You are such an asshole," he said.

"Thanks buddy, I love you too," I replied. "I'm glad you're okay. I'll check back with you later."

It took weeks, but eventually we learned Ed was a member of a bank robbery squad in Miami, which was plagued by a series of violent crimes. Two brutal thugs, former military enlisted men, had robbed several banks and an armored truck. They'd shown a vicious side and a willingness to shoot and kill witnesses and anyone else who got in their way, including the armored truck operators. They were a modern version of John Dillinger and the Ma Barker gang on steroids.

The Supervisory Special Agent in charge of the bank robbery squad apparently decided one morning that they'd had enough of the robberies, and it was time to head out and catch 'em. What he failed to take into account was that his agents were armed with handguns and a few shotguns, while Platt and Mattix were carrying automatic rifles and handguns, a critical fact they knew well in advance.

Nonetheless, out the agents went, two in each car. Several hours into the surveillance, the agents spotted the target vehicle and the driver took evasive action to lose the tail. The agents followed them into a residential area and cut them off. The four-minute shootout began as soon as Platt and Mattix leaped out of their car, firing wildly. Two agents were killed quickly and others were injured by automatic weapon fire. Critically injured, and only able to use one arm, Ed Mireles was able to load and re-load his shotgun, and by the sheer force of his will, fire his weapon, killing both of the violent criminals.

Platt and Mattix were pronounced dead at the scene, and the remaining five FBI agents would survive. Ed was nominated for and received the National Law Enforcement Officer of the Year award. By a strange quirk of fate, we would reinstate our friendship some years later by serving together in an FBI field office. Ed was deemed a hero, and no one could dispute that definition for one of the finest agents I've ever known or worked with. He continues to disagree with that assessment. Ed's wrong.

The inquiry and investigation into the shooting in Miami went on for months, and was talked about for years.

While the official results and conclusions of the investigators were never given out to the general population of agents in the FBI, it was more than obvious who was at fault and who was wrong. The squad supervisor, in the opinion of virtually everyone in the bureau, had made a rash and impulsive decision that morning to go out and find the bad guys. The fact that the robbers were heavily armed with automatic assault rifles didn't seem to enter into the equation. Nor did the fact that his squad of agents, should they find the robbers, would be outgunned beyond any stretch of their imagination.

Many of us looked back at the training we received in the academy and pretty easily came to the conclusion that the squad supervisor had no clue of the danger he was putting his men into. Or didn't even think about it. I would hate to think the latter was true. Most of us felt he was in over his head, but was too naïve to realize it.

Our monthly firearms qualifications in the field amounted to nothing more than going to a range and shooting at still targets. There were no combat scenarios or "Shoot, Don't Shoot" situations set up for us to feel the reality of being in a true gunfight. The only ones who had a clue about these potentially deadly combat situations were former cops and military members who had faced combat. The accountants and lawyers in the bureau were at a distinct disadvantage to those of us who had faced these situations. And yet it was those people who ultimately might have been put in charge of a squad that investigated bank robberies, kidnappings, extortions, and dangerous fugitives.

The FBI somehow believed the generalist training we received in the academy was more than sufficient to give them everything they needed to deal with any situation out there. It had worked back in the 1940s and '50s, so why wouldn't it work now? Why couldn't an accountant who had worked White Collar Crime or Fraud investigations be promoted and be able to supervise agents working bank robberies or other potentially violent crimes?

It was a sad commentary, not only on the training we received, which was completely devoted to marksmanship and nothing else, but on the attitude of the bureau that any agent could handle anything. The bureau refused to change. It was back to the old days when the Texas Rangers said, "One riot, one Ranger."

We were now facing many more dangerous adversaries than agents faced in the 1930s and '40s. Everything in the world had changed, but the FBI remained steadfast that they were giving their agents the best training possible, and continuing to live with the myth that their agents were highly-trained. That was a joke and one of the biggest myths about the FBI, and many of us knew it only too well. As did many of the agents in Miami who survived.

Twenty-Seven

The First FBI Academy

My mother grew up in the 1930s when FBI agents became almost legendary for the shootouts they regularly got into with gangsters of the era. The names of the criminals are still icons in the annals of American crime. "Baby Face" Nelson, George "Machine Gun" Kelly, Bonnie and Clyde, plus the violent, infamous John Dillinger roamed the Midwest, robbing banks and killing with impunity. The hoodlums were smart enough to know that once they fled across state lines, they were home free. Local and state officers couldn't go out of their jurisdiction to make an arrest, particularly into an adjoining state. The only way they could arrest the bandits was if they returned to the state and they happened upon them with an arrest warrant or committing another robbery. And the chances of that were fairly slim.

Even if they did find the gangsters, they'd wind up in a shootout and find themselves badly outgunned. Their .38 revolvers simply weren't a match for some of the weapons they'd be confronted with. Clyde Barrow, for example, was particularly enamored of carrying a .50 caliber machine gun, so the matchup was roughly analogous to a tank against a slingshot. "Machine Gun" Kelly got his name from his favorite weapon, a Thompson submachine gun. Other gang members knew if they had superior firepower, their chances of escape and freedom were heightened. Many law enforcement officers and innocent civilians died in the shootouts.

Finally, in a desperate attempt to help state and local law enforcement officers, Congress enacted emergency legislation making some crimes federal crimes. Because banks were federally insured, the FBI could become involved and could track the criminals across state lines to arrest them.

Similarly, Congress passed legislation to make "Unlawful Flight to Avoid Prosecution" and "Illegal Transportation of Stolen Property" federal offenses. Thus, the FBI finally had a set of federal laws with some teeth to enforce in their effort to combat the specter of violent crime in the country.

Congress also decreed that robbing a bank insured by the Federal Deposit Insurance Corporation was a violation of federal law. Leading the charge of assuring the bills went through Congress was J. Edgar Hoover, the man gaining more and more fame as the director of the FBI. Hoover petitioned Congress for additional agents to combat crime, and legislation was passed to increase the complement of agents virtually every year. Crime was simply not going away, and Hoover was the only law enforcement officer in the country who seemed able and willing to provide a solution to the problems.

As his fame continued to grow, the Director of the FBI was plagued by one unrelenting and persistent predicament. He had been a government bureaucrat for his entire career in public service, but had never been an agent in the field. In a congressional hearing one morning, Senator Kenneth McKellar lambasted Hoover for the performance of the FBI, and asked him, "Mr. Director, have you ever made an arrest?" The inescapable answer was "No." Hoover was embarrassed and angered by the question, and quickly sought a solution to the problem.

Alvin Karpis was known best to Hoover and others as 'Old Creepy Karpis.' A career criminal, Karpis began his criminal endeavors at about the age of ten, running around with gamblers, bootleggers, and pimps in Topeka, Kansas.

He served time in a reform school in Kansas and escaped, only to go on a yearlong crime spree in Kansas and Missouri. Eventually, Karpis was returned to prison for car theft. While there, Karpis met Fred Barker, a member of the notorious Ma

Barker Gang. While “Ma” Barker was not a criminal herself, she badgered parole boards, wardens, and governors for the release of her boys when they found themselves incarcerated. Rumors that she ran the gang with an ‘iron hand,’ much as Hoover ran the bureau, were apparently untrue. But they were true with Hoover.

Karpis and Barker formed their own gang when they were released in the early 1930s. Their reputation grew, and they would not hesitate to kill anyone who got in their way, including innocent bystanders. The ‘Karpis/Barker’ gang was one of the most formidable gangs of the 1930s, robbing banks and mail deliveries, and soon turned to the new and lucrative field of kidnapping for profit. Two of the kidnappings netted the gang $300,000, and the gang continued to grow, reaching nearly thirty members at its peak.

With the fame garnered by Alvin Karpis, Hoover took him on as a challenge, vowing to personally make the arrest himself. Which must have been a frightening thought to his agents.

Hoover would not have to wait long. On May 31, 1936, FBI agents located Karpis in New Orleans, and upon prior instructions from the Director, immediately apprised him of the information. Hoover left immediately to be in charge of the arrest. A dozen or so agents reportedly swarmed over Karpis’ car as Hoover announced to Karpis that he was under arrest. The versions begin to differ at this point. In his memoirs, Karpis said FBI agents seized him and had him under control. Only then did the agents call to Hoover, telling him it was safe to approach the car.

The official FBI version of the arrest is at considerable variance with what Karpis claimed. FD-302s, the FBI's basic investigative report, showed Hoover being directly involved in the arrest of Karpis, to the extent he prevented Karpis from grabbing a rifle in the back seat. One problem with that version was the car, a Plymouth coupe, had no back seat.

The fiasco was further aggravated when Hoover ordered his men to "put the handcuffs on him." Not one agent on the scene had handcuffs with him, and Karpis was tied up with an agent's necktie.

Whatever the real story was, the capture of Alvin Karpis permanently placed Hoover's name into the public eye, and his name would remain synonymous with law enforcement until he died in 1972 at the age of seventy-seven. Alvin Karpis was the last of the 'Public Enemies' to be taken into custody, a galvanizing event which seemed to elevate both "J. Edgar Hoover" and "The FBI" into national prominence. Law enforcement in the USA would never be the same again.

Twenty-Eight

One Wild Class Party

On a clear, cool autumn night, nearing the end of our eighth week, we held our first official class picnic, which served as another occasion to engage in a wild, uninhibited drinking binge.

The interestingly named Lunga Reservoir is situated about a quarter mile north of the academy grounds, but light years away from the rigors of our classes and daily routines. The reservoir is usually a pastoral, serene place for military families to relax, complete with picnic tables and boats to rent, nestled among tall oak and elm trees and huge pines. We showed up after classes one Friday night ready to let our hair down.

Tom Jensen, our class counselor, had proven to be much less of a tight-ass than some of us originally thought. In fact, Jensen led the charge on several of our escapades in the beer hall. One night, he joined us in an after-hours party in our room, where the beds were stacked against the walls and the room was turned into a disco for about a dozen of the usual drunks. I chose to operate the light switch, turning it on and off to create the proper disco atmosphere. We partied that night until the booze ran out and everyone woke up the next morning with dreadful hangovers.

"Hey!" Jensen yelled at several of us gathered near a picnic table, already snarfing down the booze. "I need a couple of you guys to help me get this grill and food out of the back of the car." A few guys headed over to the car, while a few more grabbed a cold beer out of a cooler.

The academy had provided a decent supply of hamburger patties and hot dogs, with the usual trimmings and condiments and two huge containers of baked beans and potato salad. It was our job to grill enough burgers and dogs for everyone who chose to show up. Several of our classmates chose to skip the event, realizing it'd turn into a major drunken orgy. Our two Mormon classmates never attended one of our drinking bouts, and it wasn't unusual for some of the big drinkers to be arriving back at the academy at the same time they'd be getting up in the morning. I'd eventually discover there were a surprising number of Mormons in the bureau. The first two I'd ever encountered were the two in our class. A Mormon FBI agent, Melvin Purvis, was the agent who shot and killed John Dillinger back in the 1930s. Mr. Hoover apparently believed if he hired more Mormons, he'd eventually find another one like Purvis. He was also reported to highly respect the values of their church, since the Mormons were apparently similar to the church he grew up in as a boy.

By the time Jensen arrived with the barbecue grill and food, the supply of beer in the coolers was running low, and several people were well on their way to la-la land. Surprisingly, Doc and Boots were two of the most sober. "Hey, let's make a run to the liquor store at the Marine base," Boots suggested.

"We're almost out, and this supply won't last us for another hour." Doctor Frankenstein echoed his agreement with Igor, his able assistant. Jensen had grossly underestimated our classes' ability to consume great quantities of virtually anything alcoholic. He'd brought two cases of beer over on his first trip with the coolers, and we'd gone through that like piranhas on a rodent in the Amazon River. It appeared our class was ready to rock and roll that night.

"Okay," Jensen agreed. "But we all need to chip in about ten bucks apiece. Who's gonna drive? I've gotta get this grill fired up and get some burgers and dogs ready for you animals. There's some wood in there, too, so why doesn't the resident pyro get a campfire going?" He looked around. "DeCamp! You seem like the most likely candidate, since you've got about every other perversion known to man."

"Thanks, boss," Gary replied sheepishly. He raised his arm and flailed his wrist limply. "I never thought you noticed, you big silly boy." Jensen looked at him, grimaced, and shook his head.

"We can take my car," Boots volunteered. "I'll head over and get it and in the meantime a couple of you can collect the money. Doc and P.J., how about you do that and be ready to roll by the time I get back? I think the base liquor store closes at seven p.m., and I sure as hell don't want to drive into town. Plus, the prices are a lot better and we can get a hell of a lot more booze."

Boots took off toward the parking lot as Doc and I set about collecting a ten spot from those in attendance. When everyone had contributed their share, we had about two hundred dollars.

"What're we supposed to get?" Doc asked, and everyone began chiming in.

"Get some vodka."

"Get some whiskey."

"I want some scotch," said Jensen.

"All right, all right," I replied. "Trust us, we'll get some good stuff, but we'll definitely pick up a decent supply of beer. Most of you characters will drink that."

The trip took about an hour, and when we returned Jensen and a few of our classmates had most of the meat grilled and the table set up with food and condiments. Our arrival was greeted with a cheer as Boots backed his car in and opened the trunk.

"Holy shit!" someone shouted. "Did you guys buy everything in the store?"

"We even got some ice and cups," Doc announced proudly, as we started hauling the booze out of the trunk and onto an awaiting table. A few cases of beer were dumped in the coolers, so we were restocked and ready to go again.

Jensen looked into the trunk. "Damn. Are we supposed to drink all of that tonight?"

"Who knows?" Boots answered. "But I'll bet we can put a pretty good dent in it. We done good, huh?"

By the time we all finished eating and cleaned up the mess, a half dozen or so of us gathered around a picnic table with Jensen. Boots and Doc were roaming around the campfire, slurping down the booze while looking for some sort of useful activity to become engaged in while remaining in a state of stupor.

"Hey, Tom," I said to Jensen. "I was talking to a guy in the beer hall a few weeks ago and he was telling me about ol' Hoover and his boyfriend. What's the story with that?"

"That's old news, P.J. All of us who've been in the bureau for more than ten years had our suspicions about Mr. Hoover and Clyde Tolson."

Gary DeCamp said, "Well, those of us who've been in law enforcement before coming in the bureau hadn't ever heard about it. Was it something that was kept pretty close to the vest inside the bureau?"

"I suppose it was," Jensen replied. "Mr. Hoover had so much wood on people that no one would say anything disparaging about him or his personal life. Not that he didn't have his critics, mind you, but to even suggest he had some sexual quirks could put someone from the press or politics in a very sticky spot. And they all knew it, so it was pretty much one of those *wink wink* situations. Everyone *knew*, but no one would say a word."

"So why is all this stuff just starting to come out now?" I asked.

"Hard to say. The bureau was like a family with a dictator for a father. Whatever happened in the bureau stayed inside the bureau. He was all about the saying 'don't embarrass the bureau,' so even if an agent pulled something stupid, it never got outside the field office. And most people in the field didn't have a clue why an agent was suddenly transferred to Butte or Fairbanks. A lot of guys pulled some pretty stupid stuff, and the boss was swift and certain with his discipline. No questions asked."

"Such as?" asked Nicole Jackson. "What did you have to do to get yanked out of your office and sent to some faraway place?"

Jensen said, "All I know is some of the stuff I've heard about. I was in a big office, Chicago, and you wouldn't believe some of the things guys would pull. We had an agent who was selling Amway products on duty time. Hoover put him on the applicant squad for life. A fate worse than death for most agents. Another guy had his wife using his bureau car to take his kids to school in the morning before he left for work. That wasn't a real good idea, either. Another one was using his bureau car to haul hay for his horses. It's pretty much an old axiom in the bureau that the three ways to get in big trouble are the three B's—booze, broads, and bureau cars."

"Those things don't seem like they could get you transferred, though," Gary said.

"Yeah, but there was plenty of other stuff. An agent and his wife were at a swinger's club one night, and when they left, some dumb ass pulled a knife on 'em. So the agent pulls out his roscoe and puts about three rounds right into his chest. No problem with the shooting, but when Hoover found out where they'd been that night, he canned both of 'em. It was just one thing after another. Agents are human too, you know. We had more than a few agents screwing their informants. It just goes on and on."

"Stuff you just never think would happen in the straight-laced FBI," I commented, shaking my head.

While this conversation was in progress, several of us watched as Boots and Doc amused themselves climbing a nearby tree. And we then heard the medical marvel say, "Hey Boots, let's go take a boat ride."

"We can't do that," Boots said, his tongue thickening and his words beginning to blend together from the booze.

"The guys who rent the boats aren't there and the boats are locked up, you drunken lunatic."

"Don't sweat the small stuff, Boots. I'm sure we can figure out a way to get one out on the lake. C'mon. You ready?"

"Hell yes!" Boots joined Doc, and the two drunks staggered toward a short wooden pier where five or six boats were chained to the dock.

I was sitting across the table from Jensen, and Slipper Toomey had joined us. Being more of a long distance runner than a sprinter when it involved drinking, I was nursing a vodka and tonic while Jensen had a cup of scotch on the rocks. Toomey, apparently another lightweight drinker like me, was sticking with beer.

"Those two dumb asses are gonna get us all in deep shit," Slipper said. We could see the Doc kneeling down on the pier, working diligently to dislodge a chain from its attachment on the wooden deck.

"Nah," Jensen slurred. "They'll never get one of those boats loose."

"Don't count on it," I said. "My roommate's capable of almost anything, none of it good."

Jensen said, "Yeah, he is a piece of work. He and his boy Boots were up at the beer hall one night and I saw the Doc literally crawling out of the elevator. He had a full pitcher of beer in his hand and didn't spill a drop."

"The boy's got skills." Slipper laughed.

"Yeah," I replied. "Like that night when he was out until lord-knows-when and then flunked the First Aid test. We'd spent half the night studying that useless crap, and we had it down pat at about midnight. We were all pretty much ready for the test and passed it. But after we finished studying, it was too late to drink anywhere here at the academy, so the Doc took off into town. Next thing I know I'm trying to wake up what smelled like a microbrewery. I have no clue when he got back, but he probably didn't get an hour's worth of sleep."

"Hmmm, I always wondered what happened with that test." Jensen took a sip out of his cup. "Doesn't surprise me, though. I was on duty one night when I got a frantic call that he and Boots were trying to get into one of the women's rooms. Heaven knows what that was about, but she was frantic with the two of them out there trying to beat the door down. I threatened to recycle both of 'em to one of the classes behind us, but I don't think that had the slightest effect on either one of 'em."

Suddenly, we heard one of the maniacs yell, "We got it loose, now what do we do?"

Slipper started laughing. "Hey, look! Those two whackos got that boat loose from the pier. Look, they're using their hands to paddle the damn thing over here."

"Oh my God." Now Jensen was laughing, too. "I just hope the marines who run the concession don't show up. They're gonna have a shit fit tomorrow morning when they open up for business. If they put two and two together and realize we were having a picnic here tonight, we're all going to be in front of the Assistant Director on Monday. We'd better clean up good so there's no sign of us being here and maybe they'll never figure it out."

Someone in the crowd said, "Look at 'em. Doc's gonna flip that damn thing and toss both of 'em in the lake." By now, the dynamic duo had paddled up to shore with their hands and leaped out of the boat. "We gotta take it out on the lake." Our resident physician's speech was clearly excited despite his inebriated state.

"How in the hell do you propose to do that?" Boots wandered toward our table and grabbed another beer.

"Gotta get some good paddles," Doc replied.

"They don't have paddles," someone said. "They have motors on the back."

"All right you assholes." Doc leaped onto the table. "We got some paddles right here."

"Where?" Boots looked even more confused than he should have been.

"This table. We got some planks. Let's take 'em off and we can paddle that thing across the lake."

Slipper had a tool kit in his car, so he headed over and opened the trunk, returning shortly with a set of socket wrenches. And just as quickly, the Doc was under the table loosening boards. Next thing we knew, as we stood around watching, Doc and Boots had a quite creative method of moving the boat through the water. They raced back and jumped in. The Doc pushed off from shore, they got into deeper water, and both of them started paddling like hell. In short time they were in the middle of the lake.

"Hope those morons don't drown," Slipper said.

"If alcohol floats on water, they're safe," Gary DeCamp replied.

We lost sight of the two psychotic seafarers as they paddled to some unknown destination. "Out of sight, out of mind," Nelson grumbled. "Now we can do some serious drinking without those two distracting us with their crazy antics."

That lasted for about a half hour. It was a bit of a problem sitting at a table missing a couple of planks, but we managed. Next thing we knew, someone shouted, "Here they are." Sure enough, right back to the shore they came. And then both jumped in water right up to their necks.

The crowd gathered around our two well-oiled classmates. Tom Jensen told them, "Hey, you two idiots are soaking wet. You better take those clothes off before you catch pneumonia or something worse."

"Yeah, I am getting cold," Boots babbled. "Get the campfire going a little better and we'll see if we can get these pants dried out."

Someone threw a few more logs on the fire and the two reprobates stood as close as they could, shivering, swilling their beers, and gaining some measure of heat from the intensity of the burning logs.

"This is gonna take forever," Doc complained. "And we're gonna freeze our asses off. Let's go back to our rooms and change. I'm soaking wet and I don't think we'll ever get dry standing here."

"Good idea," Boots said. They both began staggering through the trees toward the parking lot where Boots had parked his car after delivering the booze. "We'll be right back. Don't drink all the beer." And away the terrible twosome went.

Jensen, Toomey, and I returned to our conversation. "What are those two ne'er-do-wells gonna pull next?" Jensen asked.

Little did we know.

The noise level decreased as the crowd diminished in size, and even more while the two class pranksters were gone. By nine o'clock we'd lost quite a few of our classmates, and only those of us who were the more committed partiers remained. Which may have meant eight or ten were left. We stoked the campfire and sang a couple of horrible songs, all the time pouring more booze into our alcohol-ravaged livers. While there was plenty of high-pitched laughter, the scene around the campfire was much more serene without our resident physician and his scalawag intern.

Then suddenly, without the slightest warning, the entire group around the fire was startled by loud war whoops from the pine trees behind us. Everyone turned as two naked forms emerged from between the thicket of trees, running at full speed toward the group and the fire. Doc was followed closely by his favorite playmate. In a flash, still whooping and hollering, Doc headed straight for the fire, leaping straight through it on a path to the lake. Boots followed, also hurdling the dwindling fire with an athletic leap, fortunately avoiding singeing any lower hanging body parts.

That was enough for Jensen. "It's probably time to start getting this place cleaned up," he announced. "Let's see if we can clean it up to the point there is no sign of humans having been here tonight." Most everyone got busy picking up empty beer cans and tossing them into bags, and then into the back of Jensen's car.

At about the time we were cleaning up, Doc and Boots returned from another dip in the lake. Naked as jaybirds, they both started trying to repair the table, and miraculously returned it to its original state. In their state, that had seemed impossible.

Having done sufficient damage, Doc and Boots returned to the crowd around the campfire, stood there in all their glory slurping down yet more beer, then beat a hasty retreat back into the trees. They emerged dressed a few minutes later.

"All right!" Doc yelled when they returned. "It's time to do some serious drinking."

"Serious drinking." A classmate laughed. "Both of you dumb-asses are about as shit-faced as you're going to get."

"Hell no," Boots responded. "Tomorrow's Saturday and we can sleep our hangovers away. Let's get some booze and get with the program, you bunch of pussies."

Everyone there, myself included, had drunk more than our fair share for the night. "Let's get outta here," Jensen said. "If you guys want to get a few beers, go ahead and grab 'em out of the cooler. We need to get going before the Marine base police show up here and haul us off to the brig."

And off we went, back to the dorm and a chance at a peaceful night's sleep. Or so we thought.

While we could lock the doors to our dorm rooms, most of us didn't. "Why do that?" a classmate once said.

"Who's gonna steal your shit, an FBI agent? C'mon." Tonight that would prove to be a small oversight.

I was sound asleep when the door to our room flew open, slammed against the wall, and made me sit straight up in my bed. "Hey P.J., get up. It's party time!" Doc's unmistakable voice shouted as I rolled over with bleary eyes and the first signs of a hangover.

"What the hell are you doing, you crazy bastards?" I knew I could speak in plurals, because if you saw Doc, Boots probably wasn't too far behind. I looked at the clock. It was 4:15 a.m. "Jesus Christ, go to bed. I'm dying."

"C'mon, P.J.!" Boots yelled. "We need you. We've still got a cooler of beer, and we need some help drinking it." "Forget it, Boots. I'm sure you guys can do fine all by yourselves. Just keep the noise down. I've had all I need to drink tonight." I turned over and covered my head with the pillow, certain it was the last time I'd go out drinking with those booze heads.

I was, of course, wrong.

Twenty-Nine

Theft of Bird Guano Cases?

I turned my head slightly to the right and looked at the Doc out of the corner of my eye. It was something of a '*Did he just say what I think he said?*' moment. Doc made an odd facial gesture, twisted a corner of his mouth upward, and raised his eyebrows. Both signs indicated to me that he was as incredulous as I was.

Mr. Young, our instructor, had said, "Now, I want to cover some of the more obscure statutes we enforce, but they're still on the books. So we still enforce 'em."

The violation we were shocked about concerned "Theft of Bird Guano from the Aleutian Islands," a chain of islands off the coast of Alaska. He continued, "Anyone who removes bird guano from the Aleutian Islands is subject to imprisonment for up to one year, and a fine of ten thousand dollars."

I was sitting there thinking, '*Surely you're kidding me here. If I wind up in Alaska, I get to arrest people who steal bird shit from rocks? This is a violation the renowned FBI investigates? And I'm supposed to take this seriously why?* Thus my glance at the Doc, and his back at me.

Up to that point, the session had been pretty interesting. George Young was someone we hadn't seen since the second or third week of our training. His role then was to instruct us on the history and culture of the FBI, and to extort us into reading one of the most boring books I'd ever read: *The FBI Story*. And worse yet, to do a book report.

Young's function in our tenth week was to review some of the statutes enforced by FBI agents around the country. He continued with his canned lecture. "Over the years, Congress has enacted hundreds of federal criminal statutes. The FBI can use only a few of these in its daily enforcement activities. In any given year the FBI will use quite a number of these laws as the central charge, but the overwhelming majority of bureau cases are brought under only a few dozen statutes.

Young again began reading from his prepared script. "A person who is charged with criminal offenses as a result of an FBI investigation rarely is accused of violating only a single law. A drug dealer, for example, might be charged under separate laws concerning the illegal distribution of drugs, money laundering, and racketeering. Similarly, a crooked government employee might be charged with fraud against the government, mail fraud, and criminal tax violations." He looked out at the class and, having no apparent questions, continued his lecture.

"Many federal statutes mirror local ones. This means, for example, that FBI cases involving such matters as bank robbery, kidnapping, and truck hijacking could also be brought by local authorities. One result of this situation is that every time the FBI involves itself in an investigation that could be handled by city or state police, it has less time for matters that are better addressed at the federal level such as national security and the criminal violations of large corporations."

Young paused after having read a considerable amount of text. "Any questions?"

Gary DeCamp raised his hand and asked, "Mr. Young, are we going to be arresting people for stealing bird shit and for not having doors taken off their refrigerators?" Young had also cited the federal violation involving refrigerators after reviewing the bird shit statute.

Several of us either laughed or muffled one.

"Let's put it this way," Young replied. "If it's on the books, we might have to enforce it. I will say this, it would not be a high priority case that we'd go out on patrol looking for. I mean, I'd hope you'll have a lot more to do than drive around in Alaska looking for guano violations. Or to even drive around looking for refrigerators sitting outside that have doors on 'em. It's a problem, you know, kids crawling inside and suffocating. But I'm afraid we can't solve every problem in society."

Young returned to the body of his lecture. "The FBI is the principal investigative arm of the Department of Justice. It has the authority to investigate specific crimes assigned to it. The FBI is authorized to provide other law enforcement agencies with cooperative services, such as fingerprint identification, laboratory examinations, and police training."

Again, he looked at the class. "Any questions about this?" There appeared to be none. Things had rapidly deteriorated to the level of boring, and I could see Doc was catching a few Z's.

Young returned to his lecture notes. "We investigate several types of white-collar crime including health care fraud, fraud against the government, and bank fraud cases." He shuffled some papers at the podium and switched to a slide with a bunch of unreadable small text. "Okay, what I want you to do now is look at the third page of the handout I passed out. Everybody got it?"

Apparently we all had it in front of us.

"This is the Manual of Investigative and Operational Guidelines, or MIOG, section dealing with bank fraud investigations. If you look at the first part, it talks about the ways a report will be made to the FBI. Most often it will be the Federal Deposit Insurance Corporation making a referral. That will come to you as an assigned case. Does everyone see the example of that on the next page?"

We all looked at a full-page face sheet of an FDIC referral form as Young continued.

"When you get this form, your responsibility is to do three things. First, you send a Letterhead Memorandum to the U.S. Attorney's office to advise them you have a case so they can open a file. That document needs some basic, general information concerning the referral from FDIC. Secondly, you send a letter to the FDIC, which acknowledges receiving the referral. And finally, you must send a letter to the bank on official FBI letterhead. This letter advises the bank that the FBI has opened an investigation, and may also cite the name of the investigator who will be contacting them. All of this must be done in the first thirty days after receiving the referral." Again he looked up. "Any questions?"

Later, several of us gathered in the hallway after dinner and our workouts. Our studying had ground to a halt, since virtually all of our testing was finished after the twelfth week. We would, however, have another test over the federal statutes George Young had been covering and would cover more in the ensuing days.

Jim Nelson posed the first question. "Does anyone get the feeling that if we don't follow the MIOG to a 't', we're going to find ourselves in some serious trouble in this outfit?"

"Sounds that way to me," Gary countered. "But I know one thing for sure, I'm going to be all about working the bird shit cases." Which got a pretty good laugh.

"I can't believe that," Nicole Jackson joined in. "When people think of the FBI, I think they believe agents are out there getting in shootouts every day. Maybe even one or two on the way into the office every morning. Now we're starting to find out what the *real* FBI is all about."

"It looks like a frickin' paper mill to me," Dark Clark chimed in.

"No kidding," Willie Austin said. "And let's say doing written work is not one of my strongest areas."

"If they've got some pre-printed Letters of Censure sitting around," I commented, "they might as well just plug my name into a dozen or so, because I'm not one to read an instruction book before I do something. Take those bank fraud cases. If I get a referral from FDIC that someone's embezzling money, my nature isn't to sit down and write a bunch of letters. I was a cop too long to be that passive about things. I'm on the bank like ugly on an ape."

"But it sounds like you're leaving yourself hanging out there if you don't follow the MIOG to the letter," Gary retorted. "Do we have to do the same thing with a bank robbery? That's all about taking money, but with a gun instead of a pen."

"Good point, Gary," Willie said. "I can just imagine getting into a chase on a bank robbery and telling my partners, 'Whoa boys, I need to write a letter or two here.'" Which also got a good laugh.

"I don't know about that," Nelson responded. "But some of this crap makes me nuts."

I shook my head. "You can't possibly get anything done if you've got to sit down and write a letter to the U.S. Attorney's office, a teletype to the bureau, and heaven knows what else. Some of this stuff can't wait until all of these approvals get shuffled around at the bureau and Department of Justice. Could take days. I don't understand all of the slowdowns we've got to face. How in the hell are we supposed to do our jobs if we're sitting at the desk writing a bunch of bullshit paperwork all day?"

"Hey, P.J. Where's your buddy Don Bishop been lately?" Nicole asked. "I haven't seen him around since we did the shotgun training with the Remington."

"He's got one of the new classes, so I suppose that's keeping him a little busy. I haven't really seen him in a few weeks, other than to wave at him in the chow hall at lunch. He's a great guy. Someone who definitely gets it. I just hope I can hook up with someone like him when I get out in the field."

Thirty

The Boardroom: Home Sweet Home

Supervisory Special Agent Don Bishop and I had become pretty close friends and confidants by the time we were in the latter weeks of our academy training. He seemed to appreciate the fact that I'd been in the battle during my years as a police officer in California. That gave me some credibility with him.

I also admired and respected all the years he'd spent in the bureau. Don was stationed in the Dallas office when President Kennedy was assassinated. He'd been through some wars I couldn't even begin to understand, and I appreciated the years he'd served and the things he'd seen over all his years as an FBI Agent.

One night when we got together in the beer hall, he said, "P.J., you have no idea what you're getting into. I could blow some ice cream up your ass and tell you the FBI is all it's cracked up to be, but I can't. I've got to tell you the truth. You're young and you're a smart guy, but you simply can't imagine what you're getting involved in. The FBI has probably run this country since the nineteen forties. Do you realize that?"

"Well—not really," I stammered. "I always figured the bureau was all about guys like Efrem Zimbalist, Jr. and the rest of the agents out there kickin' ass and takin' names. Arresting bad guys."

"I hate to disabuse you of that, P.J., but someone has to tell you how the cow ate the cabbage. You know what I mean?"

"Probably not. I suppose when I applied to the bureau, all I thought about was some of the cases the FBI has been involved in over the years. I remember when I was just a kid in Colorado, some guy named Graham blew up an airplane leaving Denver. I don't remember all the facts, but I remember the story about how the FBI broke the case. If I recall, this guy Graham took his mother to the airport in Denver and put her on the plane. Then he went to some place where he could take out a bunch of insurance on her and applied for a large amount of money. Two hundred thousand dollars, I think. I'm not sure about the amount, but it must have been a hell of a lot of money back then. Still is, I suppose. Do you remember that case?"

"Oh yeah. Big time. There were about forty people killed when the plane left Denver and suddenly exploded over some city north of Denver. It was a United flight I think. I was in Dallas when it happened. Brand new agent. My SAC sent a bunch of us to Denver on a 'special.' That's what we called 'em back then. If some big investigation required a lot of agents, Mr. Hoover would dispatch a bunch of us to work the case. It seemed like we had a lot of specials back then."

"So what happened?" I asked.

"I wasn't in charge of the whole case," Don said, "but I was certainly involved. So I probably knew most of what happened. Something about the wreckage, maybe the smell of the luggage, told some of our guys that an explosive was involved. So they decided it wasn't an accident pretty quickly. Some people had bought life insurance for their relatives before they boarded. One of them was a guy named John Graham."

"Okay, that's it, I remember his first name now, I said. "I think he went by Jack though. Is that right?"

"I believe you're right about that. He turned out to be the guy who did it. We spent thousands of hours doing background checks on all of the passengers on the flight, and all of their relatives." He waved his hand in an all-encompassing, swooping motion and continued. "One of them had some problems with his mother and I think he'd been arrested for fraud, or something like that."

"That sounds right to me," I said.

"So it seemed Graham had some sort of a grudge against his mother. Stuff she did to him in his childhood, I think. Apparently he hated her. Our guys looked into his background and found out he was the beneficiary of her will, and a couple of insurance policies. The more they looked at the guy, the better he looked as a suspect. If I remember right, they searched Graham's house and his car. I think they found some bomb making parts which were like the ones they sifted out of the wreckage. Long story short, he copped out to putting a package in his mom's suitcase that contained dynamite and a timing device of some sort."

I grimaced. "Cold hearted son of a bitch!"

"No question about it. Kills about forty people for some money. But Mr. Hoover loved talking about the investigation. Solving that case gave the bureau more publicity than they ever could have imagined. Put the fear of God into some bad guys, probably. Gave us quite a reputation."

"So what happened to Graham?"

"They fried his ass. I think it took about a year of court hearings and stuff and boom. Greased him. It was pretty quick as I recall. Back then, they didn't screw around. The lawyers didn't have all of the appeals and other crap they use to slow down the courts now."

"You got that right. I can imagine some of the changes you've seen over the years."

"I just wish things were the same as they were back then," he said. "Once the Supreme Court started handing down decisions, it was boom boom boom. Gotta tell people they can have an attorney present. Gotta get search warrants even if we arrested someone in a house. On and on and on. Everything went to hell in a hurry. All of a sudden we've got a bunch of lawyers telling us what we can and can't do. It was hard as hell for a lot of us who'd been around for so many years."

"Yeah, Don, I can believe that, but you know cops and agents are pretty smart," I said. "It might take us a little while, but we can figure ways to get around a lot of that legal mumbo jumbo."

"I agree, but one of the problems we've always had in the bureau is having so damn many lawyers around. I'm sure you know there was a time when Mr. Hoover would only hire lawyers and accountants. Some of 'em thought their job was to be a lawyer instead of agent. Couldn't make a damn decision unless they did all sorts of legal research. So you've got a dangerous guy with a gun in his hand. You just don't have time to do all the lawyer crap. There's got to be a decision in a split second. If you even hesitate for a second you've got a bullet in you."

"Very true. Been there a couple times myself."

"How those people survived the old days, I don't know. A lot of 'em just stayed in the office. Scared to go out on the street. You've probably got a few in your class."

"Might have more than a few!"

"Well, P.J., it's a new era."

"I'm starting to get that picture."

"Hell, we can't even shoot at fleeing felons. No warning shots or anything. They might as well take our damn guns away. Make it like it was back in the thirties."

Jim Nelson and Nicole Jackson joined us just as we were ordering another pitcher.

Don continued after he greeted both of my classmates. "And now, things are only going to get worse. We've got this director, Webster. What was he, a federal judge? Missouri or someplace. Just another lawyer who is clueless about what an FBI agent has to do. The only time he sees one is when the agent is testifying in court." The pitcher arrived and Nelson poured a glass for each of us, then went up to get another one.

"Have you guys got any good information on him yet?" Nicole asked.

"Not a lot, but he's probably going to be an empty suit. He's got a bunch of law clerks in his office up there at the puzzle palace, so he probably wants to run the outfit like it's a big law firm. And now our guys are going to sit around reading a bunch of Supreme Court decisions? Gimme a break. We don't have time to do that crap. We'll never get anything done if we're trying to play lawyer all the time."

Nelson returned and, hearing the last comment, said, "It's getting a lot more complicated, isn't it?"

"Complicated isn't the word for it. Every office has one of these legal advisors now, so the SAC can't do a damn thing until he runs it by the legal staff. The lawyers have the outfit by the neck, and it's only going to get worse with this new guy. Mark my words."

I shook my head. "You've gone through a lot of crap since Mr. Hoover died. A bunch of different directors and all sorts of other changes. I've gotta give you credit for that." Don took a swig of beer.

"Tell you the truth, that's why I'm back here teaching firearms classes right now. Things were getting so bad out there in the field with all the bullshit we had to do, I just couldn't deal with it anymore."

Nelson said, "Well, you certainly get some credit for surviving it all."

"No kidding. Ain't been easy, though. I've got a few more years left here and then I pull the pin. Hang up the old six shooter and head off to the fishin' hole."

"Can't say I blame you," Nicole said.

"Don't get me wrong," Don continued. "I'm not bitter about a thing. I've really enjoyed my time as an agent. Of course, I'm not one anymore, but it sure had its moments. I've talked to a lot of guys about it as they get close to retirement. They all agree the bureau takes every last drop out of you. And then they cut you loose and wait for the new crop to arrive. Like you guys. It's just a vicious cycle. You'll see exactly what I'm talkin' about in twenty years. Most of you will figure it out after five years or so."

A few more of our classmates wandered into the room, looked at us and headed over to the table. Nicole issued a stern warning. "Don't even think about sitting down unless you're bringing beer."

"Yes, ma'am," Boots said as he, Doc, and Gary DeCamp turned and headed for the bar, soon to return with more pitchers of whatever was on tap. The three of us chatted aimlessly until the other three joined us.

"Whatchu guys doin'?" Doc asked.

"Just bitching a little," Nicole responded.

"Should be easy for you," Gary kidded, as Nicole raised a finger to one of her favorite tormenters. Nelson got us back on track. "So Don. Tell me this. What was it like when Mr. Hoover died? I mean, what happened after that, speaking of changes?"

"Well, simply put it was chaos," Don said. "Total confusion. None of us knew what the hell to do. We had a couple of assistant directors who wanted to take over and it was a mess for all of us. Big power struggle. Hoover had been there so long that we suddenly didn't have a clue who to follow. Granted, he was a crazy old guy in a lot of ways, but all of us knew what to expect."

"Must have been like the king dying." Nicole was one of the few women in the class who virtually all the male agents respected. Born in Germany, she graduated from Penn State with a degree in psychology, and eventually got her master's in Criminal Justice at Michigan State. Relatively small in stature, Nicole more than made up for her lack of size with an aggressive attitude not unlike a wolverine. She was a fierce opponent in defensive tactics, and was always far ahead of the other women in our two-mile runs. In fact, she always finished well ahead of more than a few of the men, including me.

"Not a bad analogy, Nicole," Don said. "As crazy and intimidating as he was, he could flat run the FBI."

"Hmmm." Nicole took another drink of her beer. "I didn't think about that. We're all coming in under Judge Webster as the director, and that's who we're going to get used to, I suppose."

Don looked around the table a few times, sipping on his beer. "You guys don't have a clue what you're in store for with Webster. The senators who confirmed him were in love with the fact that he was a former judge. Which is a crock, since that has absolutely nothing to do with his ability to run the FBI. But after Watergate, they were looking for someone who was squeaky clean. Didn't matter that he had no idea what it meant to investigate a case. As a judge, he'd just see this in a vacuum."

"In reality, Don, how much of an effect is he going to have on us?" Nelson asked. "I mean, we're just little minions out there trying to do our jobs."

"You're somewhat right, but when more of this legal business starts filtering out to the field, you'll see it affecting what you do and how you do it. It's already hard to get anything done, but it's gonna get a whole lot worse."

"Such as?"

"Okay, let me give you an example. Rumor is, we're going to start getting involved in drug cases. Let's say you've got an informant who can call his dealer and set up a delivery. P.J., you were a cop, what would you do?"

"That's easy," I said. "We'd get him on the phone and record the call. Get the deal set up and do it. Did it all the time. You mean we can't do that?"

"That's right. Not unless there's a huge emergency involved, and there rarely is with a drug case. What you've got to do is call an Assistant U.S. Attorney and explain the case to him. Then you need to send him a letter to confirm his opinion that making the call is a good idea. Then—and this is the fun part—you've got to send a teletype to headquarters explaining the whole case to them all over again. That goes through a desk at the bureau, upstairs to the legal unit, and then they're going to have to run it past someone at the Department of Justice."

Nicole looked incredulous. "Geez Louise. All of that red tape just to make a phone call. It could take a week."

"Yes, ma'am."

"Something's telling me they don't really want us to work drug cases," Gary offered.

"If that's the case," Nelson added, "how in the hell are we supposed to get anything done?"

"That's the big question," Don said.

Gary said, "I know how I'd get it done. I wouldn't say anything to anybody. I'd either just do it or I'd have an officer from one of the local agencies get it done for us."

"Which is a great idea until your office gets inspected."

"And then what happens?" I asked.

"If you have any paperwork in your file about the call, but you don't have all the other confirming paper, you're in deep shit."

"Oh my God," Nelson said. "Letter of Censure time."

"Can't you just plead ignorance?" Nicole asked.

"Forget it. They figure when you get out of the academy, you know everything you need to know. And if you don't know it, then you'd better look it up in one of the manuals. The MIOG and MAOP are the bibles of the bureau." MAOP was the acronym for the Manual of Administrative Operations and Procedures.

"Reading instructions isn't one of my strong suits," said Gary. "I'm the worst person in the world to build a swing set."

"Better get used to it," Don responded, looking around the table at all of us. "When you're done here, you're accountable for everything you do."

"Even if we're not trained to do it?" Boots finally showed some awareness of the conversation. He and the class brain surgeon had been down at one end of the table slurping down beer as fast as they could, trying to figure out where to do even more drinking when the beer hall closed.

Doc finally joined the conversation and made his first profound statement of the night, which sounded roughly like a garbled, "Yeah." And then went right back to his glass of beer.

Don looked down the table at the twin drinking machines and chuckled. "At least I can see some of you've figured out a way to survive this place."

"Some of us, hell," Gary said. "This class is a bunch of booze hounds. Well, we've got a couple of Mormons and a few others who won't consider drinking, but for the rest of us it's balls to the wall. No other way to endure this crap."

Draining his glass and setting it down, Don said, "It's all gonna catch up with us one of these days. Hoover set the agenda for this academy way back in the thirties, and it hasn't changed a lot since. Even after he died. The people in the upper echelon are all old Hooverites, and none of 'em see any reason to change things. Now we've got Webster, and he's not going to have any idea about what happens down here for new agent training. I don't see this place ever changing."

Thirty-One

Willie the Golden Gloves Champ

Willie Austin had become something of an icon in our class. Nothing or no one seemed to bother him, and he seemed impervious to pressure. Or if he felt it, he certainly didn't show it. Even on the pistol range, where he was a horrible shot, Willie seemed to let his scores blow right past him and everyone else. Somehow, he knew he'd improve to the point where he'd pass and graduate from the academy. Or if he didn't, he never said so.

At six foot five and about an order of hash browns under 250 pounds, Willie was an imposing figure in more ways than one. His black, well-trimmed hair and reddish complexion left no doubt of his ancestry, and he was proud of it. He endured the nicknames of 'Chief,' 'Savage,' 'Tonto,' and others, laughing it off and handing the abuse right back. Willie was a man's man in every possible way. As the old baseball player and announcer Dizzy Dean said, "He could hunt bear with a switch." Willie Austin was a pretty impressive guy.

If anyone thought Willie got in the bureau under Judge William Webster's Affirmative Action plan, they had another think coming. Growing up the hard way on a reservation in New Mexico gave Willie some insights into life and people none of us had. He was as sharp academically as anyone in the class, and he didn't drop a step to any of us in matching wits away from the classroom.

Our challenge in the twelfth week was completing Defensive Tactics. There were certain skills and holds we had to master and show we could complete on an adversarial subject. In other words, someone we were going to arrest who didn't want to be arrested, and who wanted to kick our asses. We needed to know how to put handcuffs on the suspects 'the right way,' and not backwards so they might hurt the person we were arresting. We needed to show we knew some holds that would control a suspect who was resisting, but not to the point he'd get injured. And finally, we needed to show our instructors we could fight with a person who challenged us.

We also had our final two-mile run to complete, as well as the Agility Test and Physical Training Test. It was destined to be a busy couple of days, and the possibility of some people getting washed out still loomed over us.

Since Willie Austin and I were two of the bigger guys in the class, we were often paired together in defensive tactics drills. Which struck me as odd, since the smaller women weren't under a guarantee that everyone they'd arrest would be their size.

For our final drill, we were all told to don football helmets and boxing gloves. The drill was to control an 'arrestee' in a physical confrontation. The exercise was designed to engage people in the class who had never been in a fight in their lives. Willie and I were not among that group. He'd fought his way through school on the 'res', and I'd pretty much done the same in the mostly blue-collar town where I'd grown up in Colorado. Plus, I'd spent ten years as a cop, and if you don't get in a fight or two a week, you're probably not doing your job. Neither he nor I were the type to back down from a fight if there wasn't another option.

I looked at Willie as I donned my headgear. "Don't worry," I said with a laugh. "I'll be easy on you." He nodded. I wasn't worried. I don't think he was, either.

"Ready," our instructor said. "Fight." We danced around for a few seconds and I took a swing at Willie, which he blocked, then countered with a jab to my face mask. An easy jab. I took a better swing at him and he countered with a right cross to the left side of my helmet, which knocked me unconscious and flat on my ass. The next thing I knew was I was looking out of the ear hole of the football helmet as I woke up on the mat.

"P.J., you all right?" Willie asked, offering his hand to help me get up. The instructors raced over, and everyone in the class had stopped to look.

"I think so." I was still dizzy and motioned that I'd just as soon stay right where I was for a minute or two.

Our instructor stopped by to check on me. "You going to be okay?"

"Oh yeah. I should be good to go, just as soon as I get my head re-attached to the rest of my body." I looked up at Willie. "Damn, bitch, what the hell did you hit me with?"

Willie just shrugged his shoulders. Later I'd find out why.

That night at the beer hall, I talked to several of the guys about getting my lights knocked out by Willie. "I've never lost a fight in my entire life, and that includes ten years as a cop. He put me out like a baby in a rocker in about thirty seconds."

"Hey, P.J.," Slipper Toomey said. "Did you know Willie was the New Mexico State Golden Gloves heavyweight boxing champion when he was eighteen?"

"Oh my God. That's a big surprise. Now I know where the truck that hit me came from."

At my expense, everyone got a few laughs about Big Willie's KO, as well they should have.

Jim Nelson entered the discussion. "Can you believe the results of the physical training? That gal who was a teacher in Philly…they're gonna throw her ass out, I think."

"You got that right, Jim," echoed Gary DeCamp. "It's fun to watch her run with those big boobs flapping up and down, but she smokes like crazy and she didn't come anywhere near sixteen minutes on the two-mile run. Probably closer to twenty minutes, and she was walkin' the last half mile."

"Big shock," Doc chimed in. "There's a few in the class who did the agility test in thirty seconds or so. I could do it in thirty seconds walking with a beer in my hand and a cigarette in the other."

Willie said, "Yeah, Doc. But you'll have to admit, you were a bit of an athlete in your day."

"Well, not that good of one." Doc was being diffident. "But if they set up some standards for this crap, then why don't they stick with 'em?"

"What did you do on the agility Doc?" Nelson asked.

"I dunno, fourteen seconds or something. How about you P.J.?"

"Right at eighteen, Doc, but I've got a few pounds on you."

Carl retorted, "But at least you've been working out and running. That broad with the huge boobs hasn't got out on the road and done a damn thing."

"Probably not." I shook my head.

"But you know the guy who amazed me is Chip Taylor," DeCamp said. "When I first got a look at that guy, I thought 'no way Jose.' No chance of him ever making it. He musta been close to the Willie line in weight, and he's not quite six feet tall. That guy was a porker, but he's worked his ass off."

"Hey Gary," Willie protested. "You better watch that 'Willie' crap, or we might have to step outside!"

"Whoops, sorry Willie." Gary cringed in mock horror. "You will only hear me sing your praises for the rest of our careers. I don't want to wind up in la-la land like P.J. did."

Thirty-Two

Preparing to Meet the Director

All right you jokers, shut up and sit down." Tom Jensen had to shout over the din in the classroom on the Thursday afternoon of our thirteenth week.

We all quieted down and turned toward the podium. It'd been an enjoyable week for most of us, but not for some others. We lost a few more classmates during Physical Training Week, and the people who were gone probably shouldn't have been there in the first place. They'd either been misfits and didn't fit the 'FBI Image,' or had done so poorly on their PT drills that it was clear they had no business being an FBI Agent. One had flunked firearms, even though he'd been given numerous remediation opportunities and chances to pass. When you can't shoot above 50 percent on the range, no one would want you out there as their partner. I'd had a good final qualification with a 99.6 percent, which meant I just barely missed the 'Possible Club.'

"Tomorrow, we're going up to Headquarters to meet with the Director," Jensen said. "Here's how it's going to work. You need to be up for breakfast and getting ready after that, because we're leaving here at nine o'clock sharp. No excuses or late arrivals. If you're not in the circle to meet the busses, your goose is cooked. We'll arrive at HQ about ten a.m., and they'll have a tour of HQ set up for us. That's going to take about two hours, and we're heading down to the cafeteria for lunch at noon. At one o'clock sharp, we'll get together and head up to meet the Director.

He's planning to meet with us at one fifteen." He looked out at the class. "Any questions?"

Willie raised his hand and Jensen acknowledged him. "When we meet with the Director, are we supposed to just sit there, or can we ask questions? I don't think any of us has the slightest idea of what's supposed to happen."

"Good question, Willie," Jensen replied. "Back in the old days when we met with Mr. Hoover, our meeting with the Director was pretty much the final step in the selection process. If he thought you were too fat or too skinny, maybe too ugly, or if you were bald or your hands were sweaty, he'd tell the counselor to fire you. On the spot. No questions asked or answered."

There was a dropping of jaws and an almost universal "Ohhhh" in the class. Everyone was thinking the same thing. *We got this far, we passed all these tests and did all the academic work, the physical training and firearms stuff, and now this guy can fire us because he doesn't like how we look.*

"It's a different story now, but you have to understand, this is the first time I've met the new director myself. So for all I know, he might can me right on the spot." Jensen looked out at the class, expecting a laugh, but didn't get one.

"This guy is all about Affirmative Action and has more of a humanitarian side to him than Mr. Hoover did. Since he's fairly new, we haven't seen him do anything like the things Mr. Hoover did. But that's part of the problem. We just don't know."

Gary DeCamp asked, "So what are we supposed to do? This whole 'Meeting with the Director' sounds a little ominous."

"Okay, good question. You all need to be in your best dress clothes, shaved cleanly, hair trimmed and looking good. For you ladies, same thing. I'd recommend you have your hair up and your makeup just right. Again, we don't know what this guy will do or what he thinks is important.

So all I can say is do your best to look your best, and you'll be fine. Any more questions?"

No hands were raised. We probably were all feeling a little intimidated, if not in complete terror, at that point.

That night, several of us made the usual pilgrimage to the beer hall, having nothing else to do and nothing stressful the next day. Sid Talbot, our primary firearms instructor, was there along with several other instructors from the Firearms Training Unit.

Jim Nelson asked, "So what do we know about the new Director?"

"Well, let's put it this way," Sid replied. "He's a judge and he's probably going to run the bureau like he ran his courtroom. He doesn't have the slightest idea what our jobs are like. I'd suspect he thinks like a lot of people do that every agent is trained to do every single thing. And all of us old timers have started seeing some changes. Because he's a lawyer, I think he wants all of us to know as much about the law as lawyers do. We've already started to see a lot more court decisions and legal garbage being sent out to the field."

"Sounds like we've got some big trouble on the horizon," Gary said.

"Ya think?" one of the other firearms instructors responded. "Webster was appointed by President Carter, who is a complete limp dick. He's an engineer, which is about as clueless as you can get. A total detail person. I talked to a friend of mine with the Secret Service who told me Carter schedules the tennis courts at the White House. I mean, c'mon, the guy is the leader of the free world, and here he is making tennis reservations. Carter just doesn't get it. So he's the one that appoints the new Director of the FBI. Figure out how that makes any sense."

"Really," Sid said. "And you wonder why interest rates are going through the roof, and we've got hostages in

Iran. He has no idea what to do, and he's the guy appointing our new boss. It's gonna be ugly. Luckily, we've got a new president on the horizon, I think. If anyone votes for Carter over Reagan, they're crazy as hell. Carter is a complete bonehead. He's a well-intended one, but a bonehead nonetheless. He might go down as the worst president in the history of the U.S.A."

"What does all that mean for us?" Willie Austin asked.

Sid looked at Willie, and then the rest of us. "It means a lot. He's the guy who provides you with leadership in the field. He tells every SAC what his priorities are, and if they don't follow what he wants, their personal evaluations suffer. So they adopt his priorities."

"Which are?" I asked.

"Good question," another firearms instructor answered. "Right now, we don't know, but what we do know is if an agent gets in a firefight and shoots someone, he's going under the microscope immediately. It's happened already. Webster will assume the agent is in the wrong, which is complete bullshit. He's a lawyer who's probably watched a lot of John Wayne movies, and believes the agent is supposed to shoot the gun out of the bad guy's hand. He doesn't understand why an agent would ever get in a situation where he has to shoot at someone, even if the guy has a gun pointed at him."

"We've got some big changes to make in this outfit," Sid said. "It's not the old days anymore. Hoover was hung up on the thirties and forties. None of us believe he was willing to change the training. He didn't and it hasn't changed very much, and there's a possibility it never will. Maybe some minor adjustments. It's like Hoover was saying, 'Our training was the best back then, and it still is. We're training our agents the way we need to train 'em.'

"He couldn't get beyond that, but things are very different now. We've got gang bangers out there with some serious guns in their hands and they'll shoot you in a heartbeat. And there are a lot more of 'em than there were the old gangsters in the days Hoover was used to. It's the 1980s now and we've got to make some serious changes in this academy or we'll be even farther behind than we are. This is supposed to be the premier law enforcement academy in the world, and we're anything but. LAPD and Sheriff's Office both have academies which are much longer, and in which they don't teach their officers useless stuff like we do."

"Director Kelley understood that," yet another instructor chimed in, "but this guy Webster has been in a courtroom forever, playing judge, and has no clue what it's like out on the street for our agents. If someone thought major changes needed to be made at the academy, the palace guard up there would feed Webster a line of bullshit and tell him everything is just fine the way it is. And this is going to go on forever. Why? Because the guys going through training now, for the most part, have never been through a law enforcement academy like some of you guys. The likelihood of any of you winding up as the Assistant Director of the FBI Academy is between slim and none. So it's never going to change.

"If our guys get in a gunfight, they're going be completely outgunned by these characters we've got on the streets. Some of our bosses have met with him and told the director we need to go to semiautomatics, but he doesn't understand what we're talking about. It isn't gonna be fun when some of our guys get in a real shootout with some serious bad guys. Even then, he's never been out there, so he probably won't ever get it."

"Holy crap," Willie Austin said. "It sounds like we'll be out there with pee-shooters against big-time guns."

"You got it, baby," one of the instructors replied. "All we've got to do is lose some agents and things might change. But 'change' is the operative word here. Webster is clueless about what's happening out on the street for our guys. It's a sad state of affairs for all of us, and not just with the guns we use. The training here hasn't changed a hell of a lot from the nineteen forties. And the problem is, Webster has a huge learning curve. He doesn't know that we're still training our new agents to catch the guys in the old gangster days. He's got more important things to do than worry about the academy. And so will the person who replaces him, and the next guys down the line. I'm just concerned we will never change things back here, and you're going to be getting a few more useless weeks like you did with fingerprinting and first aid. How much have you learned about conducting an investigation? Virtually nothing, except they tell you to check the MIOG to see what you need to do. We're really bullshitting the general public when we tell people how 'highly-trained' we are. If they only knew."

It was getting near closing time, and we began to fill everyone's cups to have one last beer before heading to our rooms. Sid took a drink and said, "There really hasn't been much of a change in the training for new agents since most of us went through the academy in the old post office building. Sure, this place looks great, but it's all for show. Someone needs to begin to understand just how poorly we're equipping our new agents to go out in the field. And I don't just mean guns. I mean a complete overhaul. But I'll bet twenty years from now, there won't be an appreciable change and our agents are going to hit the street with no training in when to shoot and when not to shoot. How to make arrests. That stuff in the gym you guys do is crap. I'm just glad I've got most of my time in now. I would not want to hit the streets and have to face what you guys are going to get thrown at you. No thanks. I'll just stay here until I retire."

Our group was pretty quiet as we walked through the halls and took the elevator up to our rooms. Willie said,

"Hey guys. I've got a couple of quarts of some good stuff in my room. Anyone up for a quick one?" He didn't have to wait long for an answer.

Thirty-Three

A Brief History of FBI Directors

The position of FBI Director, while not a Cabinet appointment, is one of the most important in the government bureaucracy. It is important, influential, and critical to the security of the country, not to mention being a driving force behind the agents in the field who work daily with state and local law enforcement officers in solving complex crime problems.

Over the one hundred years that the FBI has been in existence, seventeen directors have managed the agency, with varying degrees of success. Of those, eleven were lawyers and one was a certified public accountant.

The first director, Stanley Finch, took his post in the summer of 1908. His mandate was to deal with the problem of 'white slave traffic' in the United States. Congress and other politicians felt the country was plagued by foreign women in the brothels of America. For his appointment, Mr. Finch could thank many women's groups who apparently thought these 'jobs' should have been reserved for American women only.

Mr. Finch served until 1912. His administration was marred by corruption, which should come as no big surprise since most of his agents were dealing with matters involving prostitution.

Finch's successor was Alexander Bielaski, who served from 1912 until 1919. He was supposedly kidnapped for ransom in Mexico during his term, but escaped his captors with the ransom money in hand. No one is quite sure how that happened, and suspicion centered on

Bielaski's own involvement in the kidnapping plot. When he resigned, he went on to work as an undercover agent in a Manhattan, New York, speak-easy. Everyone involved with government at that time suspected foul play in his kidnapping and new job, but since nothing could be proved, he went on to live in relative obscurity.

Bielaski's replacement, an Assistant Director by the name of William Allen, served as the Director for only four months before William J. Flynn arrived on the job. A burly former Secret Service agent, he served from 1919 to 1921 and was heralded as the greatest anarchist chaser in America. No one is quite sure what that meant, but most presume he had a vendetta against dissidents, and also had the authority to deal with the problem due to his position and power. He also didn't last long.

A former FBI agent, William J. Burns, was next in line to be the Director of the FBI. During his time as an agent, Burns had gained a reputation as an 'international crime investigator.' He was an energetic and fashionable man who chose to wear vested suits decorated with gold watch chains and a black derby. Rather than growing to fight continuing crime problems, the bureau shrank under Burns' watch, from its 1920 high of 1,127 personnel to 600 agents and support employees in 1923. His suspected involvement in the Teapot Dome scandal of 1924 led to his resignation. Burns later went on to found an internationally known detective agency, which still exists today.

The agency's sixth director was Justice Department attorney J. Edgar Hoover, the unquestioned face of the FBI for forty-eight years. He led the FBI through eight White House administrations, babying and bullying his agents and Congress at times, but ever relentless to serve his country. Some questioned if the notion of 'serving his country' was as true as serving himself and his own organization, but Hoover was the consummate bureaucrat. As one older agent once told me, "The old son of a bitch could flat run the FBI."

Hoover was the son of two civil servants, a native of Washington, D.C., and was a person of strong and pronounced convictions. He felt Christian morality was the core of American values, and he harbored a deep distrust of anyone who called those values into question.

He was an overachiever who worked days at the Library of Congress and earned his law degree from George Washington University, completing his degree at the age of twenty-two. Upon graduation, he went to work as an attorney with the Department of Justice and quickly gained his reputation as an anti-Communist by directing the arrests of over four thousand people whose views were anti-American.

At the ripe age of twenty-nine, Hoover was offered the job of Director of the FBI. He quickly charted a course to turn his agency into a well-oiled machine, by standardizing both hiring practices and techniques for conducting investigations. The arrests and convictions of notorious gangsters such as "Machine Gun" Kelly by his agents brought considerable fame to the FBI. "Baby Face" Nelson, at the time of his arrest, was said to say, "Don't shoot G-men," forever memorializing the FBI agents who'd confronted him with overpowering firepower. The FBI was chronicled in the media and on screen as the heroes of American society. And Hoover did nothing to dispel the myth.

Because of the successes and capture or shootings of outlaws and bank robbers, the bureau's powers were broadened and it was renamed the Federal Bureau of Investigation in 1935. Hoover continued to make changes, expanding the field of domestic intelligence and the fingerprint files in the Identification Division. The effect of this was to compile the largest collection of fingerprints ever, and to solve hundreds of crimes by using print comparisons. Hoover also created the FBI Laboratory in 1932, which was originally designed to examine evidence found by the FBI, but now serves all law enforcement and is regarded as the preeminent forensics laboratory in the world.

Initially, Hoover's concern was in dealing with subversive activities and groups. The FBI spied on thousands of suspected dissidents and radicals in the United States. While Hoover clearly exaggerated the dangers posed by some groups and individuals, Congress bought into Hoover's beliefs and the perceived threats to the country. Indeed, President Harry S. Truman once commented, "The FBI kept us from sabotage during World War II." Little did Truman or Congress know that most of the *successes* supposedly racked up by the FBI were by pure, unadulterated luck, as well as information furnished by foreign intelligence agencies.

Hoover also fought what seemed to be a never-ending battle with famed Washington Post columnist Jack Anderson over the existence of La Cosa Nostra, the notorious Mafia, in the U.S. For years, Hoover had rejected the possibility that such an organization existed. Well-placed sources, however, provided Anderson with irrefutable evidence that the scope of the Mafia's crime network was immense in the country, even extending into Cuba. Finally, in 1956, Hoover's own agents interrupted a meeting of high-level Mafia members at a remote cabin in the New York foothills. By identifying those present and providing the information to Hoover, he was finally convinced the Mafia was a threat which needed to be addressed. And reluctantly he did.

Thousands of previously classified FBI documents released by the Freedom of Information Act show Hoover maintained a list of over twelve thousand Americans suspected of 'disloyalty' to the United States. Many believe former Wisconsin Senator Joseph McCarthy, the American architect of exploiting the fear of communism, received a considerable amount of his information directly from Hoover.

Hoover's increasing concern with radical groups led to the formation of a *dirty tricks* program now known as COINTELPRO, an acronym for Counter Intelligence Program. Initially directed at the Communist Party, COINTELPRO was later extended to focus on groups such as the Black Panther Party, Martin Luther King and his Southern Christian Leadership Conference, the Ku Klux Klan, and many others.

On March 8, 1971, while much of the country was watching the Muhammad Ali-Joe Frazier fight, a two-man FBI Resident Office in Media, Pennsylvania was burglarized. When agents arrived for work the next morning, they discovered file cabinets in the office had been virtually emptied. An anonymous group, later identifying themselves as "The Citizens' Commission to Investigate the FBI" was credited with the crime, although it was never solved. Over a thousand documents were stolen, and COINTELPRO became major news and an equally major embarrassment to the FBI.

The objectives of COINTELPRO were relatively simple: Infiltrate organizations with undercover operatives and informants; commit burglaries to obtain information; use illegal wiretaps; plant false evidence and documents; and to spread false rumors about key members of the targeted organizations.

Following the revelations about COINTELPRO, politicians and the press had a heyday leveling charges and allegations against Hoover and the FBI. A select Senate committee declared the activities of the FBI to be "illegal and contrary to the Constitution of the United States." Hoover was roundly criticized for failing to investigate the murders of civil rights workers, but was able to regain some good standing with the American people following the arrests and conviction of Klan members in the case known as "Mississippi Burning."

President John F. Kennedy's assassination in November 1963 was a galvanizing event for Hoover and the organization he had so skillfully crafted in his own image. At that point in its history, the FBI had thousands of so-called *security cases* open on citizens across the country, an important information-gathering component of the COINTELPRO program. Agents in the field who were working such cases were required to report on the activities of these individuals every ninety days at a minimum. Lee Harvey Oswald happened to be one of these people.

With the power wielded by Hoover, the role of the FBI in the investigation was a prominent one. And Hoover personally oversaw every phase of the investigation. In 1979, seven years after he died, Hoover was excoriated by the House Select Committee on Assassinations in a report which was critical not only of the FBI, but the Warren Commission and other agencies involved in the investigation. Claims were raised that Hoover had information that would have cleared Oswald of involvement.

Several presidents, including Truman, Kennedy, and Lyndon Johnson, considered firing J. Edgar Hoover. However, he weathered these and other storms when all of the presidents concluded that the political cost of firing Hoover would be too great. Reportedly, Hoover's close ties with Congress and the belief he had considerable dirt on the presidents caused them to realize firing him would be detrimental to their own ambitions.

J. Edgar Hoover was a brilliant man who staked out his turf and built an organization in his own image. Some may question his motives and methods, but no one can deny that Hoover created a myth and mystique about the FBI. He steadfastly refused to allow negative information about the bureau to be publicized, often blackmailing media members with the files he was reputed to maintain. And probably did. It seemed to Americans that the FBI was an omnipresent institution in society, and a force to be forever reckoned with.

Thirty-Four

FBIHQ Tour and Meeting the Director

My first thought as we sat down in the Director's conference room was, who else has been in this room? Presidents? Generals? Certainly Attorneys General, and maybe an occasional Supreme Court Justice. Politicians? Movie stars? The table was huge – roughly the same size as the deck of a Midway-class, World War II aircraft carrier. The chairs were comfortable, dark blue cloth, and plush. There was plenty of room for everyone in the class. And probably enough room for another class.

The day started out pretty smoothly. Doc and I were up early for breakfast, met some of our classmates in the dining hall, discussed the day ahead, and then headed back to our rooms to get dressed. The bus was waiting for us in the circle behind the Madison dorm. We loaded up and away we went.

Most of us were in a festive mood, eager to get away from the academy for a day, but also excited to meet the Director and tour FBIHQ. At one point during the ride, our bus driver, a middle-aged black man, commented, "This class looks like that frickin' movie *One Flew Over the Cuckoo's Nest*. Ya'll got a bunch of whackos and a big Indian who fits the role perfectly." That comment got a pretty good laugh, particularly from Willie. Nothing bothered him.

We pulled into the basement and headed up on the elevators for our tour of HQ and the FBI Labs. As opposed to the brief tour we took on our first day, months before, this one was more in depth and actually quite enjoyable. However, it was pretty clear that some of the people in various sections of the lab saw it as a pain in the ass and would rather have stayed at their workstations examining some important pieces of evidence.

Our tour guide pointed out the various sections of the FBI Lab, but when we got to the main part of the building his voice changed into what sounded like a recorded message.

"The J. Edgar Hoover building was completed in 1972, but Mr. Hoover never got to work in the building. He died several months before it was finished. In 1972, President Nixon obtained approval to officially name the building in honor of the former Director of the FBI. At the present time, the building houses over seven thousand employees, and is over two million square feet in size. Several hundred Supervisory Special Agents, Unit Chiefs, and Assistant Directors work inside. Each is responsible for coordinating specific violations of federal law with agents in the field. The FBI has fifty-nine field offices, all of which report directly to FBI headquarters. For the first sixty or so years of its existence, the FBI was housed down the street inside the Department of Justice building. Mr. Hoover petitioned congress for a new building several times, finally obtaining approval in 1962. Construction began several years later. The style of the building is completely unique to the Washington, D.C. landscape, much like the organization itself."

The structure of the FBI essentially begins at FBIHQ and extends out across the country to all of the field offices. At the time, each of the fifty-nine separate field offices across the country was headed by a Special Agent in Charge (SAC). Because several offices and cities were larger in size, such as New York or Los Angeles, an

Assistant Director in Charge (ADIC) led those offices, with several SACs under his command. J. Edgar Hoover designed the management structure to be fairly flat, and not top-heavy, saying once, "The work of the FBI occurs at the level of field agents, not supervisors or managers."

Following the canned tour, which was exactly the same as the general public receives, we did a self-guided tour through the FBI Museum and Hall of Fame, which honors fallen agents and highlights the accomplishments of the FBI over the years. The last step of the tour was a firearms demonstration by an agent from the Firearms Unit at Quantico. Again, this part of the tour was a replica of the demonstration received by the general public. I noted with interest that the target being used was gray and white.

The cafeteria at FBI headquarters was a madhouse. It seemed most of the seven thousand employees in the building were there for lunch when we arrived. If not, the rest showed up soon thereafter. The selections from the cafeteria were surprisingly good and reasonably priced. We all managed to find tables or to sit with some of the full-time employees. When someone hears "I work for the FBI," the listener usually assumes the person is an agent. Little do they know there are thousands of civilian employees, from fingerprint examiners to clerks running around delivering mail from one office to another. I was surprised to learn that nearly half of all FBI employees were housed in the building. At that point in history, the FBI employed nearly ten thousand agents in the field and at FBIHQ.

At exactly 1:00 p.m., we gathered at elevators outside the cafeteria and headed up to the seventh floor. We were greeted by an Assistant Director, and Jensen led us into the conference room. Judge Webster arrived precisely at 1:15 followed by several young men, who I would later discover were his law clerks. All of them stood behind him as he sat down.

"Good afternoon, ladies and gentlemen, and welcome to FBI headquarters," Judge Webster began. "I have a few brief comments and then I'll take any questions you may have. First of all, let me congratulate you for nearly finishing your academy training. We are very proud of our organization and we expect to be equally proud of the work you'll accomplish in coming years."

The Judge was a soft-spoken man, in his early 50s, with perfectly trimmed dark hair and a stately appearance. His suit was clearly expensive and everything about him radiated culture and class. "The FBI is the most well-known investigative agency in the world, and we're glad to have each of you as a part of our team. When you finish your training and go to your field offices, you'll find some challenges you've never confronted before. At this point in our history, we're doing some of the most important work in the FBI that's ever been done. I can't talk about the cases in detail, but I do want you to know some of you will be involved in those investigations. Our agents are currently working on a case which deals with corruption at the highest levels in our government."

None of us knew what he was referring to, of course, but in due time we'd all learn this reference was to the famous ABSCAM case. An undercover FBI agent, posing as an Arab sheik, met with a number of federal, state, and local politicians, making payoffs for various favors they produced due to their positions. It was the first major operation by the FBI to trap corrupt public officials, but critics later said the methods employed by the FBI were more about 'entrapment' than legitimate investigative techniques. In later years, several U.S. Attorneys General would promulgate "Investigative Guidelines" for the FBI when working these types of cases. Agents would say the guidelines made it nearly impossible to investigate such a case.

The ABSCAM investigation led to the conviction of a U.S. Senator, five members of the House of

Representatives, a New Jersey state senator, several members of the Philadelphia City Council, and an Inspector for the Immigration and Naturalization Service. Ultimately, all of the ABSCAM convictions were upheld on appeal, although some judges criticized the tactics used by the FBI and lapses in FBI and Department of Justice oversight into the techniques. Rumors in the FBI also made it clear Judge Webster was one of the critics.

Using undercover agents and techniques to investigate crime was something few in the FBI were familiar with, and made many traditional 'Hooverites' more than a little uneasy. The closest Hoover had ever come to approaching 'undercover' was allowing his agents to go without their trademark brimmed hats.

Webster said, "We have also made some significant inroads to organized crime in this country, and we expect to start seeing the results of that work within the year." Once again, none of us in the room could be expected to know or understand the scope and effect of these investigations.

In New York, Special Agent Joe Pistone had gone undercover as 'Donnie Brasco,' posing as a jewel thief. The original game plan of the investigation was to investigate jewelry heists, not to infiltrate the Mafia, but a combination of events created a 'perfect storm' of unexpected opportunities. An undercover investigation intended to last six months wound up going six years, with Pistone continuing to make contacts and collect evidence. Once he was ordered to perform a hit on another Mafioso, Pistone/Brasco was pulled out of the operation.

Evidence collected by Pistone eventually led to over one hundred indictments and convictions of Mafia members and associates. To this day, Joe Pistone remains a legend throughout the FBI for his work in undercover operations.

On the other coast, at about the same time, the FBI office in Los Angeles had launched an undercover investigation of a completely different sort. Targeting pornography dealers in the L.A. Basin, undercover agents had set up a business to distribute pornographic films in the San Fernando Valley. Cash customers were scarce until a day in late 1979 when five Mafia family members came by to pay a visit that wasn't intended to be social or involve a purchase. The gangster's goal was to lean on the business 'owners' to assure the Mafia had control of all pornography-related businesses in the L.A. area. Little did they know they were dealing with undercover FBI agents who'd rented the building and set up shop as porno dealers. Eventually, the entire Mafia family in Los Angeles was indicted and convicted for various charges including extortion.

While this was a critical event in naming the L.A. family "The Mickey Mouse Mafia," several other important events unfolded which led to the demise of the mob. Acting boss Aladena Frattiano, better known as "Jimmy the Weasel," became only the second Mafia member to break the sacred law of *omerta*, the vow of silence. Frattiano discovered there was a contract out on him from the Chicago mob and decided to turn on his associates. Ultimately, Frattiano testified against mobsters in Los Angeles, Chicago, and Detroit, with many going to jail for extended stays.

If Hoover had been the Director at the time of our meeting, one of our classmates would have been fired during the session or shortly thereafter. Tony Martinez fell sound asleep with his head tilted back and his mouth gaping wide enough to catch flies. I was sitting directly across the table from him, but there wasn't a thing I could do. I kicked Nicole Jackson, who was sitting next to me, and we exchanged sideway glances, hoping the Director didn't notice Martinez, who was out like two girls on the town. Judge Webster had to have noticed, but nothing was said. If it had been Hoover conducting the meeting, *something* would have been said.

Webster concluded the meeting with the obligatory comments about us being the "best of the best" and again welcomed us to the FBI family. "It's a unique fraternity," he said, "and there are very few of you in the world who can claim the title Special Agent of the FBI. Now, are there any questions?"

I wasn't about to raise my hand. Tony was still sound asleep, so he couldn't ask one, but a few members of the class asked innocuous, patronizing questions such as, "What do you see as the future of the FBI?"

Tom Jensen and Sam Batterson had both warned us, "When you go up to shake the Director's hand, make sure you're not sweating. Make sure they're dry as a rock in the Mojave Desert. Do whatever it takes. Wipe your hand on your pants. Hoover used to fire an agent with sweaty hands right on the spot." That didn't mean Webster would do the same, but it was what they learned from the Hoover days in the bureau, and it was better safe than sorry. We went through the required hand shaking session and were out of the Director's office by two.

On the way back to the academy, Tony Martinez was soundly chewed on by Jensen, in front of all of us on the bus. "Martinez," Jensen said, "I can't believe you did that. I was personally embarrassed, and I'm sure your classmates were too. If Hoover was still running this outfit, you wouldn't even be on this bus right now."

Thirty-Five

The Long Reign of J. Edgar Hoover

The legacy of John Edgar Hoover was controversial in more ways than political. He was a lifelong bachelor, and rumors since the 1940s have circulated that he was homosexual. His long association with Clyde Tolson gave more rise to that suspicion. Tolson was promoted to the post as an associate director of the FBI, with no prior experience as a field agent. Everything about their relationship suggested it was that of a gay couple. Questioned about this, Hoover once described Tolson as his "alter ego." They worked together, were inseparable, ate meals together daily, went to nightclubs, and vacationed together. While the relationship was 'obvious' to some, others such as eventual director Mark Felt characterized the relationship as 'brotherly.' However, upon hearing of Hoover's death, President Richard Nixon is reported to have commented, "Jesus Christ, that old cocksucker died?" Tolson inherited Hoover's estate, worth more than $500,000, and moved into his home. Tolson also accepted the American flag that draped over Hoover's casket. Tolson is buried a few yards away from Hoover in the Congressional Cemetery near Washington, D.C.

No one truly knows Hoover's sexual orientation. Roy Cohn, a famed Washington attorney who later admitted his homosexuality, believed Hoover was gay. A witness once claimed to have seen Hoover engaging in cross-dressing and homosexual acts in the 1950s. The same witness also said the Mafia had blackmail evidence proving Hoover was indeed a homosexual, and that as a consequence, Hoover was reluctant to pursue organized crime.

In later years, after his death, Hoover's opponents described him as "J. Edna Hoover." He's been the subject of humor in books and on television, not to mention movies. But while he was alive, he threatened anyone who made insinuations about his sexuality. He had files on most of his opponents, and told them so. He reportedly had extensive files about Eleanor Roosevelt's lesbian lovers, so no one knew what he had on them. Anyone who chose to bring up the issue would be countered with, "You don't know what we have on you, *do you*?"

If anyone doubted Hoover was a dictator and wielded an iron hand over the U.S. government, a story attributed to a former FBI Special Agent might dispel some of these myths. In the book *No Left Turns*, a former agent describes Hoover as a rigid, paranoid old man who terrified everyone.

As an example, Hoover would review paperwork, and would often write on the margins of reports and memos submitted to him. When one memo had margins that were too narrow, Hoover wrote, "Watch the borders!" No one in the FBI or other government agencies apparently had enough nerve to ask Hoover what he meant by the comment. Inquiries were sent to the Border Patrol about any unusual activities on the Canadian and Mexican border crossings into the United States. It was apparently a week before a staffer at FBI Headquarters realized the message from Hoover related to the margins on the memo.

J. Edgar Hoover's death in 1972 was a shocking event for FBI agents and support personnel. The figurehead and leader they'd relied upon for so many years was suddenly gone. While no one could replace Hoover, the most likely candidate was L. Patrick Gray. His credentials were impeccable. A graduate of Rice University and the U.S. Naval Academy in 1940, where he was the starting quarterback on the football team, Gray was a submarine commander during World War II and the Korean War. After his naval service, Gray attended George Washington law school, served with the Department of Justice, and was then appointed by President Nixon to be the acting Director of the FBI at the time of Hoover's death. His appointment received little opposition.

Six weeks after Gray was sworn in as FBI Director, five men broke into the offices of the Democratic National Committee at the Watergate Hotel complex in Washington, D.C. The culprits were caught in the act by Frank Wills, a security guard at the hotel.

Unaware of the burglary, and completely uninvolved, Gray heard about it from Wesley Grapp, the SAC of the Los Angeles field office. Gray called Mark Felt, his second in command, who appeared to have limited information about the burglary. The following day, Felt informed Gray the burglars had direct connections to the Committee to Re-elect the President (Nixon). One of the burglars was the head of security for the committee, and had apparently installed at least one listening device inside the committee offices. Another of the burglars was a former FBI agent.

Unsure of jurisdiction for the FBI to investigate, Gray told Felt to pursue the matter "to the hilt and with no holds barred." Gray's involvement in the Watergate investigation continued with many contacts and interviews with coconspirators in the case. Gray resigned from his post as Acting Director of the FBI after it was revealed he provided documents to John Dean, counsel at the White House, and destroyed other documents belonging to Watergate coconspirator E. Howard Hunt. Probably the most qualified person to ever lead the FBI, Gray resigned from the FBI in 1973. He was later indicted for his role in Watergate, but the charges were dismissed. Many people feel it was unfortunate that Gray was caught up in the maelstrom of Watergate and was never able to serve as FBI Director. "He was a great man," a former FBI Supervisor said. "And he'd have been a hell of a great boss. It's too bad he was involved in that stupid mess."

Following Gray, William Ruckelshaus, a long-time government bureaucrat, was appointed as the acting director in 1973 until the nomination of Clarence Kelley in the same year. Kelley, a former FBI agent and Special Agent in Charge of an FBI field office, had gone on to local law enforcement as the Chief of the Kansas City Police Department. Seemingly settled into that job, Kelley was called upon to serve as FBI Director from 1973 until 1978. He retired and was replaced briefly by James B. Adams, who served as Acting Director until the nomination of William H. Webster.

Thirty-Six

White-Collar Crime and Photography

On a late November morning, only a few weeks before graduation from the academy, I woke up and looked out the window of our room.

"Hey Doc, it's snowing!"

He growled, "What?"

"It's snowing out there. Come look. I didn't know it snowed in Virginia."

"Shut up," he grumbled. "I've seen all the snow I need to see in my lifetime. I grew up in New York. Leave me the hell alone, I wanna sleep. I've got a fierce hangover."

"I haven't seen snow in years," I said excitedly, watching the big flakes falling and covering the bare branches of trees and the ground below.

"What is it about 'I don't give a shit' that you don't understand?" He rolled over and covered his head with the pillow.

"It doesn't snow in California," I said.

"Isn't that a song?"

"Something like that. Hey, you need to get up. We've got class in a half hour."

He mumbled something that was muffled by the pillow as he rolled over in bed.

"All right, I'm going down for breakfast and I'll see you at class."

Something that sounded like "arrrrh" emitted from under the pillow. It sounded like a pirate had broken into the room and replaced my roomie.

I arrived at our classroom just before 8:00 a.m., and I didn't see any sign that Doc was present or accounted for. I raced over to a nearby office and dialed our room number.

"Hello," a voice mumbled after the sixth or seventh ring.

"Doc, get dressed and get down here. You're late."

"Damn. Tell Jensen I'll be right there."

He came steaming in a half hour late, right in the middle of our morning lecture on White-Collar Crime. The instructor glared at him, but said nothing.

"Had to see the nurse," Doc lied and sat down next to me, smelling like a refugee from the Jim Beam factory in Kentucky.

Our classes on White-Collar Crime had, if anything, been even more boring than First Aid, Fingerprinting, and a three-hour lecture without breaks on the Remington 870 shotgun. The instructor was a tall, gaunt agent with thick glasses and a pockmarked face, lacking only a green visor to complete the look of an accountant. Which he was.

"Now," he said, as we furiously took notes. "We're going to talk about financial institution crimes. You'll find these under the '29' classification in the manual. There are a number of classifications under the '29' violations, and the determining factor will be the amount of loss to the institution."

He droned on about the different amounts of loss the U.S. Attorney's office would consider prosecuting, and the process to conduct one of these investigations. "When we receive a referral, it's usually going to come from the Federal Deposit Insurance Corporation, or what we commonly call the 'FDIC.'"

No shit, I thought.

"Once we get a letter, the manual spells out exactly what to do," and he read directly from the Manual of Investigative and Operational Guidelines, the notorious MIOG, which provided step-by-step instructions for every violation the FBI investigated. "An agent has thirty days to provide a letter to the FDIC and bank, informing them we've received the referral."

So the FDIC sends us a letter and we send them a letter to let them know we got their letter. Talk about useless paperwork.

"The investigating agent is also responsible for sending a letter, accompanied by a Letterhead Memorandum to the United States Attorney's office in their district. This LHM will outline and summarize the complaint received by the FBI, and what the intended course of investigation will be, as well as the agent assigned to conduct the investigation. This must also be accomplished within thirty days."

He finally looked up. "Once the letter and LHM is sent to the U.S. Attorney's Office, the agent is responsible for contacting them within thirty days to get an opinion as to the likelihood the case will be prosecuted by their office."

I was doing the math, and thinking. *We get a complaint of an embezzlement by someone working at a bank. The embezzlement has probably gone on for a year or so, and then we get the complaint. That's taken a month or so to get routed through and assigned to an agent, who then can take up to thirty days to send several letters and another thirty days to see if the U.S. Attorney will be interested in prosecuting the person who has been embezzling money. That's another ninety days. How much more money can the bank employee steal in that period of time before an investigation is begun?*

I happened to catch Gary DeCamp's eye in the row of seats ahead of me. He appeared confused and finally raised his hand. "Sir, if we get a complaint, is there anything wrong with looking it over and just heading to the bank to start an investigation?"

Our instructor seemed perplexed. "Well, no. I guess not." He began his response in his best accountant's voice. "We have to follow the procedure spelled out in the MIOG. I don't think an agent has ever done that."

Gary looked over his shoulder at me and raised his eyebrows. Former cops in the room were used to getting a crime report and starting an investigation if the case had merit. Those of us who had been detectives usually started an investigation immediately if possible. Once the investigation was complete, and a suspect was identified, the facts went to the district attorney's office to see if they wanted to file charges.

The afternoon session was nearly as useful. The class was on photography, and each of us was equipped with an ancient Nikon camera which was roughly the size and weight of a D-9 Caterpillar bulldozer. Our instructor explained all of the moving parts, and spent about an hour or so boring us with details of the various speeds and capabilities of film which could be used.

The intent of the class was to familiarize agents with camera equipment they might have to use at a crime scene. As with fingerprint classification, I knew this was nearly as useless, because if a person had not been trained properly in the use of camera equipment, lighting, and other factors involved at a crime scene, he might blow an opportunity to record some valuable evidence.

And then he turned us loose with instructions to start taking pictures to get used to the camera. "Go around the academy and grounds and start taking pictures of anything you want. If you go up to the District this weekend, take as many as you feel like taking." He provided each of us with eight rolls of Kodak black and white film. "When we meet next week, you'll turn in the film to me and we'll get it processed for you. So if you want to play tourist up in the District, you'll have all the pictures you need."

I loaded a roll of film, checked the settings, turned the camera toward Doc, and snapped a quick picture. "You dumb ass," he whispered.

We were free to go at two that afternoon, theoretically to take pictures for the next three hours. The usual group gathered outside the classroom.

"Is the Boardroom open?" Jim Nelson asked.

"Hell, yes," Willie replied. "I just happen to know they open for lunch and stay open the rest of the afternoon. Let's go. We can take pictures of pitchers of beer up there. To hell with running around in the woods taking pictures of trees. It's snowing out there."

Thirty-Seven

A Night at the Officers Club

Our favorite haunt away from the academy was the Officers Club on the Marine base. And that's where we headed after downing a few pitchers of beer at our other favorite watering hole, the Boardroom.

The O Club was a dark, refined place with a well-stocked bar, cheap drinks, and much higher quality food than we were used to in the troughs at the academy cafeteria. Of course, we had to pay for the food, but the prices weren't bad and the selection was varied and always done with some elegance. The cooks never knew if they were preparing dinner for a general or a bunch of lower ranking officers or FBI agents. Thus, the quality was always first-rate and the meals were well presented.

"This has been a great place to hang out. I'm glad they told us about it," Jim Nelson looked around the dining room. The thigh-high wainscoting and molding on the walls was a dark mahogany, with lightly patterned floral wallpaper and plush brown carpet. Even the tables were dark, fashioned out of teak-colored wood with starched white linen tablecloths, perfectly-placed full silverware settings, and starched napkins in empty water glasses. The comfortable, well-padded chairs were covered in black leather. The foyer was equally dark, graced with a number of tastefully appointed oil paintings of Marine Corps generals and former base commanders adding to the military ambiance. Each painting was about three feet wide and four feet high, trimmed with ornate, gold leaf wood frames. A small light bulb above each painting provided just the right amount of ambient light to enable those entering the hallway to find their way into the bar and restaurant.

We'd all been there enough that we didn't really need light to navigate the hallway.

After finishing dinner, we were well into another round of drinks when Willie Austin held up a leg and yelled from one end of the table as everyone looked. "Hey, Doctor Mason! I think I hurt my knee running. Whaddya recommend?"

"Let's amputate," Boots, always Doc's capable intern, retorted. "It's your only hope, Savage."

Dark Clark laughed. "I've got a better idea. Let's amputate his head and save the rest of the body. I think it's the head that's the problem."

"Nah." Doc finally had a chance to offer some sage medical advice. "Take twelve bourbon and waters and call me in a week."

"Or just go to the back of the pack and run with the plodders," Gary DeCamp chimed in to a chorus agreement and nodding heads. Except for one.

"Hey, you." Nicole Jackson tried her best to look offended. "I don't fit into that group, you know. I outrun almost everyone at this table."

"Not you, Nicole," I replied, raising my drink. "You're making some of us look like old fat sloths out there on Hoover Road." And others raised their glasses out of respect to another member of our class we always enjoyed hanging out with.

At this point in our training, there was no question a couple of distinct groups had formed. Most of those in our group had the common denominator of being in law enforcement before coming into the FBI. Cops always have something in common, and it doesn't matter what size town they worked in. They all deal with similar problems and people, and they all can readily understand and relate to one another.

Another group hung out at the "Globe and Laurel," a pricey surf and turf restaurant in the small town of Quantico, just outside the gates of the base, more commonly referred to as "The Major's." We'd been there a few times, but I didn't really care for the atmosphere or the crowd, which was generally comprised of former marines singing "From the Halls of Montezuma" at the top of their lungs when the piano cued up the *Marines' Hymn*, or reliving the battles they'd fought in Vietnam. Or Korea, or even World War II. Which I respected, but got a little tired of listening to. Having spent four years in the navy, my impression of the mental acuity of those in the Marine Corps wasn't terribly high.

"Hey, you guys." Willie had finally recovered from his near-amputation after consuming a sufficient amount of alcohol. "Do you guys remember that day at the cafeteria when P.J. blew those marines away?"

Several in our group looked at me questioningly. I'd almost forgotten the little encounter between a headstrong marine second lieutenant and me.

"Oh, I guess it's pretty funny now. But I thought I damn near caused a riot. We were lined up for lunch ahead of a bunch of marines who had come over to the academy for some reason. Probably to use the ranges. I don't know. Anyhow, there was this guy behind me in line who started asking me about our physical training requirements to finish the academy. I thought about it a little and told him we had to do the two-mile run in under sixteen minutes, eight pull-ups, fifty sit-ups in two minutes, and probably some other stuff. Oh yeah, the inside obstacle course, too."

"Okay," Boots said. "So what was the problem with that?"

"Well, he snickers and looks back at his buddies. And then he sneers, 'That's pretty easy.' Then he looks at me and says, 'We've got to do the two mile run in under twelve minutes, blah blah blah. He goes on to jabber about some of the other physical training minimums they've gotta do to graduate from OCS. I was getting tired of listening to him."

Everyone was looking at me wondering what the punch line to the story was going to be. If any.

"So I tell him, 'That sounds pretty tough, but do you know the biggest difference between your training and ours?'" I paused and glanced at the eager faces around our table. "He looked at me with a blank look on his face and said, 'No, what's that?' I tell him, 'We've gotta have a brain and know how to use it.' I thought the guy was gonna punch my lights out."

Everyone at the table cracked up. Several marines at nearby tables looked over at us, wondering what the joke was about. Little did they know it was about them.

Doc interrupted the laughter. "No kidding. I heard it. That's exactly what P.J. told the guy. I heard every word. I'm standing right there listening and I almost died laughing. Willie was there too, and I was glad I had these two big guys around me. I thought it was time for fist city."

"I think the only reason I was ballsy enough to say what I did was that my man Willie was there," I said. "After he put my lights out in the gym that day, I figured if anyone had my back, Willie would be my guy."

"I had ya covered, brotha." Willie was starting to slur pretty badly. "You 'n me P.J. We'da taken them assholes to the cleaners."

"That's a great story P.J.," Gary DeCamp said. "I oughta propose a toast to it, but I've gotta propose a toast to something else." He was obviously about half lit up, too.

"To what?" Jim Nelson rang in. He seemed to have a pretty good snoot full himself.

"To those of us who successfully passed the greuling FBI driving test." Gary had apparently decided to completely change the topic of conversation.

Glasses were raised. "Was that the most ridiculous thing you ever heard of or what?" Nicole posed the rhetorical question, apparently willing to further pursue the new topic in even more depth.

"Now, look." Gary got even more animated, waving his hand and glass around. "I pushed a patrol car through the mean streets for more than five years, and I spent another five as a homicide dick. Last time I checked, that meant you actually had to, oh, I dunno, do a little bit of driving. In a car! You know, one of those things that has four wheels and you sit in it. So Tom Jensen has to take every one of us out and have us drive a mile or two just to make sure we can drive. What the hell was that about?"

Gary was echoing what many of us thought when we had what we euphemistically called 'Can You Drive Day.' We all lined up in alphabetical order in the parking lot near the garage, patiently awaiting our turn, and one by one our class counselor beckoned us to a battle-ravaged old Plymouth bureau car. Each of us drove out of the parking lot, turned left onto the main road, went about a mile, made a U-turn and returned to the parking lot. About two minutes of driving per new agent.

"You know," Dark chimed in. "It seemed stupid at the time, but there was probably a reason for it."

Nelson looked incredulous. "C'mon Dark. You can't be alive now and not be able to drive a car. I spent two days at the Pomona National Speedway when I went through the academy. We did all sorts of high-speed driving and even learned how to do those PIT maneuvers. There isn't anything I haven't dealt with as an officer on the street. I mean, why in the hell can't the FBI just acknowledge that? It's like unless they see you can drive, you can't drive. It's stupid, like a lot of other stuff we've had to do here."

"Not so fast, my friend," Dark countered. "When I was in the army, we had some guys from New York who'd never driven a car in their lives."

Boots, who was well on his way to la-la land, spilled his drink as he threw a hand up in the air. "Dark, it was the same in Chicago. Some of those characters who grew up in the projects always took cabs or the trains. Probably never drove a car in their life unless they stole it." He grabbed a couple of napkins and started sopping up the mess he'd made.

"Hey, watch out what you're sayin' about the brothas," Dark countered.

"Sorry, Dark," Boots slurred. "Just makin' a point."

"Point made." Dark laughed congenially, and the rest of us joined in.

We were all in a celebratory mood. Barring something of a cataclysmic event, there was no question that we were all going to graduate from the FBI Academy in a few weeks. Most of the stress we'd felt was gone. Except for a couple of former classmates, we'd passed the significant academic tests, physical requirements, and firearms qualifications. Willie and Boots were still struggling to qualify on the range, and were getting intensive training from our firearms instructor. Eventually they'd make it.

"All right, you guys. All this talkin' about driving made me think of a story." Gary seemed to be alive again. Several of us cringed and looked at one another. Gary's stories could go on forever.

Willie groaned. "Ahh, man, here we go again."

"So Gary," Doc said. "And the story would be…?"

"All right, check this out. I was training a new recruit a few years ago. So we're on the midnight shift and this guy was havin' a big problem stayin' awake. If I was drivin', the guy would fall asleep. If we stopped to write a report, bam, sound asleep again. Even if he was writing it. So it's really starting to piss me off. One night I decided I'd try something." He paused.

"Which was?" Nicole asked, motioning with her hands as if to say, *Okay, okay, let's get on with the story, Gary.*

"So the rookie parks the cruiser one night at about three o'clock. I'm writing a report on a drunk driver and boom, he falls asleep. Head nearly hits the steering wheel. Now I'm like, 'Okay, this has gotta end.' I unzip my pants and pull out my barracuda, and then I reach over and start to rub his leg. He doesn't wake up. So I squeeze and rub a little harder. He shakes his head and wakes up and he looks over at me. I'm loping my lobster and his eyes are so big they look like a damned dinner plate. Never had a problem with him fallin' asleep after that. The boy was wide awake every night."

"Gary, *you* are the biggest damn pervert I've ever seen," Willie said. "I'm glad you're not sittin' next to me."

"Yeah," Boots responded. "But I gotta say that's a pretty creative way to keep someone from sleeping. It'd work for me. That's for damn sure. Hope my roomie never does it because I'm snoring."

There seems to be an immutable chain of events set in place when a police officer tells a *war story*. It becomes something of a challenge to *one-up* the last story. It's probably a cop thing, but all officers and former officers understand it, unless they're as dumb as a bag of hamsters.

Jim Nelson jumped in. "I don't know if I can top that one, but here's another one. Nothin' about driving. True story. I'm in the station one night and they ask me to fill in for one of the dispatchers. So I put on the headphones and I'm good to go. Takes a few minutes and I get this call. Lady says, 'Office, office, you gotta help me. I needs a bambalance.' So I'm like, 'What's the problem ma'am?' She says, 'It's my baby.' I ask her, 'What's the problem with your baby, ma'am?' So she says, 'I think my baby got the Spiral Mighty Jesus.' I'm thinking, what the hell is that? So I ask her, 'Why do you think that?' And she says, 'Because my baby havin' conclusions.' I'm all about, 'What the hell is going on here?' So I send an officer and an ambulance." And he paused.

"Okay," Nicole urged, anxious for the story to conclude. "So what happened?"

"Well," Nelson continued, "turns out the baby had a cold."

"Now look here," Dark said. "There you go doggin' the brothas again."

"Sorry, Dark," Nelson replied with a smile. "Just had to tell that one."

"Your turn, Dark," Willie prompted. "You gotta have something for us."

"I can't top that stuff," Dark answered. "You guys got all kinds of cop stories. Can't beat that smack y'all got goin'."

I was sure Dark had something to tell us about his experiences in Vietnam. "C'mon Dark," I said. "You've gotta have something that happened over there. Give it up."

Dark looked around the table. "All right, all right, all right," he said. "I've actually been wondering when we were going to go into some of the supposedly famous FBI techniques for interrogation. I mean, I thought the FBI was all about interrogating people and getting the story outta them. But we haven't done a damn thing. Really disappointing."

Nicole said, "That's true. We haven't spent a second on doing interviews of people, and I'm really frustrated about that. I thought if nothing else, the academy was gonna train the hell out of us in some patented techniques for getting information out of people. But we haven't done anything. And even worse, we haven't learned a thing about how to write reports. I'm going to be as lost as a baby lamb when I get to my first office. First I don't know how to interview anyone because we haven't had any practice, then I don't know what to do with any information I somehow get. And then if I don't get it, I'll probably wind up with a Letter of Censure."

"Hey, get this," Willie responded. "I remember talkin' to my applicant coordinator in Albuquerque. He said something like, 'We're the FBI and people tell us the truth.' So I'm thinking, *This guy doesn't get it*. If a guy's a criminal and he thinks he can bullshit you, why won't he do it?"

"All right, all right, shaddup," Nelson finally said. "Back in 'Nam, we had our own way of doing interrogations."

"And that was?" Boots asked. He was still trying to clean up the drink he spilled earlier.

"We'd get a few Viet Cong as prisoners, and we'd start to interrogate 'em about all of the usual intel. Troops in the area. Tunnels. Where are the convoys? All that stuff. Whatever might help us to be ready for another attack. If you remember, we were totally surprised by the Tet Offensive on what we thought was a sacred day of the year for them. New Years, I think. Didn't bother Charlie a damn bit. Frickin' gooks kicked our asses."

Willie said, "Okay, I remember that. So what's it got to do with not training us in interrogation at the academy?"

"Yeah." Doc bobbed his head up and down, nearing a state of stupor.

"Actually, everything," Nelson said. "We had some pretty reliable techniques. And let me tell you something. They'd get the job done over there. Can't use 'em here, though."

"So what were they?" Dark looked perplexed.

"Pretty easy. Let's say we've got three gook prisoners. I'd tell one of my chopper pilots to take 'em up to about twenty feet. But the gooks didn't know how high they were up. The Huey would fly around a bit so they probably thought we climbed to a hundred feet or so. One of my interpreters would go up with 'em and he'd start to interrogate 'em. First guy would probably say nothing. Nada. Tough little shits. I had a sergeant who was about the size of North Dakota. If not bigger. Mean son of a bitch. Anyhow, if the first guy isn't telling us anything, my sergeant would grab him by the neck and hold him out of the side of the chopper. He'd tell the Cong to give it up, so he'd tell us something, and the Hulk would drop him like a sack of rice. Boom. Down he'd go, and the other two are watching. Shitting their pants. So the second guy would tell us a few more things, and then my guy would let him sail, too. Finally, the third guy sees his boys joining the Viet Cong airborne and figures it's in his best interests to give it all up. So he's telling us everything he knows. Ho Chi Minh's sex life. You name it. And then my gorilla would just nod his head to tell him 'thanks' and let him fly, too."

"Oh, man." Nicole looked like she was in shock. "I didn't need to hear that. Omigod." She had her hands up to her face and looked like she was going to throw up. "That's horrible. I can't believe we did that stuff over there."

Nelson and DeCamp were laughing their asses off. Gary said, "That's the funniest damn thing I've ever heard. I have no clue how we apply that to what we're supposed to be learning back here, but it's the craziest story I've ever heard in my entire life."

"You guys are so gross." Nicole winced, still reeling from the story. "I just can't believe you threw those guys out of the chopper. That's horrible."

"Can't make that stuff up," Nelson chuckled.

After a quick trip to the bathroom for unstated reasons, which most of us guessed involved losing at least part of her dinner, Nicole rejoined the living again. "C'mon you guys. We were doing fine with some of those stories. I don't want to hear any more about the Flying Wallendas, Viet Cong branch."

Doc seemed to be revived after Nelson's story and rejoined the conversation. "Okay, now check this one out. I dunno if this is as bad as Nelson's story, but it's pretty nasty. "We had this brand new troop commander coming to town. He gets there a couple days early to look around, checking out schools and houses, all that stuff. They're in the middle of doing all that when he and his wife stop and pick up some chicken and head over to a park for a little picnic. They're eating and he's gotta go to the bathroom, so he sits down in a stall and starts taking care of business.

Next thing he knows, some guy in the next stall is slipping his schwantz through one of those holes in the partition. Of course our boss had his name tag on, so he pulls it off his shirt and sticks the sharp point right through the guy's prick."

"Omigod." Nicole looked like she was about to have a heart attack. "That's worse than Nelson's story. No it isn't. Well, maybe it is. I think I need to make another trip to the bathroom. You guys are complete pigs."

Gary was cringing and laughing at the same time. "Doc, you are not a well person. That's so bad I'm sitting here in pain just thinking about it."

"Me too," Willie said, putting his hands under the table in an apparent gesture of sympathy. "So what did the guy with the needle in his noodle wind up doing?"

"I don't know. Our captain said the fag was screaming when he walked out of the head. But think about it. What were the guy's options? Can't pull it back through the hole or it looks like a shrimp filet. So he winds up being at the mercy of the next guy to walk in the bathroom, I guess."

"Hey, Willie," Boots said. "If you'da flunked the First Aid test like the Doc did, you coulda done some quick surgery to help the guy."

"Yeah, just what I'd need for the tribe to promote me to Medicine Man. I don't need that kinda pressure."

Nelson looked like he was going to die laughing. "Can't make that stuff up," he repeated.

Nicole said, "Didn't you just say that?" She had a fair amount of booze as most of us did.

"Doesn't matter," I replied. "Jim's right. There is no way in hell someone could come up with those stories unless they actually happened."

"So what happened to the fruitcake, Doc?" Nicole asked.

"Our boss stood guard at the door for a while, but the guy was screaming bloody mercy. Finally, after a few minutes, he went back in and pulled the nametag out."

Thirty-Eight

Our Last Two Weeks

The last two weeks we'd spend at the academy were by far the least challenging. We'd completed all of our tests, and the remaining sessions were more about odds and ends than anything else. The pressure was off. Now it was all fun.

My greatest fear in our firearms training had been shooting the Remington 870 shotgun. For some reason I had a shotgun phobia, but some practice on the range had made me much more comfortable with the powerful weapons.

Don Bishop met the class one afternoon at an outdoor, covered classroom. "Here's what we're going to do today," he began, displaying one of the many shotguns in a rack in front of the class. He quickly racked the gun several times to reacquaint us with its operation and to demonstrate it was not loaded.

"We're going to spend the afternoon shooting skeet, or clay pigeons if the word 'skeet' isn't part of your vocabulary. We'll be using bird shot loads, but I want all of you to understand that this weapon, even with bird shot loads, can kill you in a heartbeat." He loaded five shells in the gun, racked a round in the chamber, turned and pointed the gun down range where a single target was standing.

"Skeet loads are like a whole bunch of small bb's packed into each shell. Because they're lighter than a slug, you'll have more drop and you need to aim a little higher. Also, the shot will disperse in a wide pattern, so these loads are not effective at a distance. All right, put your ear protection on." He took aim at the target and fired all five rounds in the shotgun. "Okay, everyone follow me down range."

The target was punctured with about ten small holes, none of which was in the kill zone. "At fifty yards," Don continued, "these rounds are basically worthless. All they'll do is scare the hell out of someone. Now, move behind me at the twenty five yard line." He reloaded the shotgun with five more rounds and then fired two rounds. It was easy to see that many more pellets had hit home. "Much more effective here than at the fifty. Can everyone see that?" We all nodded.

"All right, let's move up to the seven," he said. "I'm going to fire the last three shots here, and I want you to see what the target looks like when I'm done." He fired off the last three rounds, which tore the center out of the target, leaving a gaping hole. "So what did you learn from this little demonstration?"

"Don't mess with a shotgun?" Willie responded.

"Well, that's certainly true," Don said. "But there's another important point I hoped to make here. Anyone get it?"

"If you're at close range," Gary DeCamp replied, "it's effective with those rounds. If not, the weapon is basically useless."

"Exactly. Now, grab those shotguns and boxes of ammo and we'll head over to the skeet range."

The clay pigeons flew all afternoon, and we each shot about fifty rounds. Our success ratio was mixed, and it was exhausting. But it was also excellent training on being more familiar with the shotgun and its capabilities.

Several of us went out for a run that night, lifted weights, and headed up for a late dinner.

"Is your shoulder as sore as mine is?" Boots asked.

"I'm dying, big time." Slipper Toomey reached over to rub his. "That was a hell of a lot of shooting. But I'll say this. If I had any concerns with being able to handle a shotgun, that's over with for me now."

"Same here." I rubbed my right shoulder just like Slipper had. "This thing is going to be bruised as hell tomorrow, but I don't care. I was scared to death of the shotgun before I got here, now I think I'd feel more comfortable with it than I do my revolver."

Gary agreed. "I'm not sure about the slugs, but give me a few rounds of that double ought buckshot and I'm good to go. That's one bad ass weapon."

"I'm glad that bullshit in the pool is over with," Jim Nelson said one night while we were gathered in the officers club. "Does anyone know what that was supposed to be about?"

Slipper laughed. "I got the same training when I was in navy boot camp, and it was useful then, but this was ridiculous. Since when are FBI agents supposed to be Navy SEALs or some such thing? That was ridiculous."

"You got that right," Dark Clark echoed. "Scared the shit outta me when I had to jump off that frickin' tower. I don't know how to swim. Brothas don't swim. You dig? How many of us have you seen swimming in the Olympics? You hear what I'm sayin'?"

The discussion we were having during the drinking session centered around a day in the academy swimming pool. A fiftyish academy instructor with an apparent fetish for the Vietnam War, which had ended years before, had conjured up a day of the most senseless training we'd have in all our weeks in the academy.

We gathered bright and early one morning and were outfitted with army dungaree pants and shirts. Willie and I thought we'd get out of it, because we were the two biggest guys, but unfortunately for us they found some for the full-figured guys. Tight, but they fit.

The first part of the drill was to jump off a twenty-foot high tower into the deep end of the pool. And not just once. Three times. The saving grace was that non-swimmers could wear a life jacket, which were available for everyone. Most of us who *could* swim opted out of a vest, as the sudden contact with the water would force the vest into our faces, potentially breaking our beaks.

"That was torture to a brother," Dark whined. "My knees were knocking so bad I was bleeding."

I'd done a lot worse than the tower during my submarine training, so it was nothing more than a minor annoyance to me. But the rest of the day's session seemed even more nonsensical. Jumping into the pool from the side, we were instructed in how to remove our pants, tie the ends into a knot, and then use the pants legs as improvised water wings. Sort of a Polish life vest. Then, using the pants as a floatation device, we had to swim from one end of the pool to the other.

After learning this new skill, the next part of the equation was to swim around the pool with the inflated pants while carrying a plastic M16-A1 rifle.

"Hey, you bozos don't get it," Gary said. "If we ever decide to invade Minnesota it might come in handy."

"Yeah, right," Jim Nelson quipped. "By the time you get across one of those lakes, your ammo would be so damn wet that you'd have to throw rocks at the bad guys. Let alone getting your dumb ass carried away by the damn mosquitos."

"That was stupid all right," Willie said. "But how about the canoes? Was that ridiculous or what?"

"Shoulda been right up your alley, Tonto," Dark shot back. "I thought you red brothas were all about canoes."

"Fat chance, Dark. The only river we've got in New Mexico is the one down south that the wetbacks swim across. It doesn't even rain where I'm from."

Our final challenge that day had been to get into an aluminum canoe from the water. But not just any canoe. An overturned one. We were split into four person teams. Our job was to use the water wings to swim across the pool to the canoe, then turn it over and all climb into it. Without using the sides of the pool. With minimal instruction on how to accomplish our goal, it seemed to be more of a team-building exercise than anything else.

It didn't work.

Since the men had superior upper body strength, it was fairly easy for them to get the canoe turned over, and for one of us to crawl in over the side as two teammates held the other side. But it was considerably more difficult for the women. We had to work like crazy to pull them inside, all the while being *careful* not to grab ahold of the wrong places.

Willie jabbed Doc in the ribs. "Hey Doc, you and Boots needed this training before you stole the boat that night out at Lunga."

"What boat?" Doc looked around in mock innocence questioningly.

"Whaddya mean, what boat?" Boots screeched. "You like to drowned me, you drunk bastard."

"But the big question is, why in the hell did we do that training in the pool?" I asked. "Do we get assigned to the Coast Guard? Maybe get sent over to fight the Iranians in a canoe? I don't get it."

Dark shook his head and took another swig of his beer. "I think they were just tryin' to wash out the brothas. No pun intended."

"We're glad you made it Dark," Nelson replied. "You were looking good out there flapping your wings around like a drowned chicken."

"Yeah, Nelson," Dark snorted. "Just like you after an hour of chasin' the deer the other day. I thought your ass was gonna have the big one boy. You were hurtin' pretty bad."

Dark was referring to an afternoon during the week where we all got to 'chase the deer.' The *deer*, in this instance, was one Al Boccacio, the director of the FBI National Academy. Bocaccio was a workout freak, built like the Incredible Hulk without the green paint, and probably in the best shape of any fifty-year-old man I'd ever seen.

Our goal that day was for any member of the class to catch up with Boccacio, who had been given a head start of a quarter mile. But we never did. Several of our sprinter-types took off like bats out of hell, but Boccacio simply sped up to match their pace. The longer we chased him, the longer we had to run. Most of us began to peter out around the two-mile mark. But Boccacio pressed on as Tom Jensen, in a car behind us, exhorted the slower runners to catch up. Willie and I were dying. Nelson and some of the others had given up at about the three-mile mark, panting and walking. It was torture. An hour after the chase began, Jensen came along and told us to take a shortcut back to the stairs on Hoover Road. Boccacio was standing there and didn't appear to have broken a sweat.

"And the purpose of that chase was what?" Nelson asked.

DeCamp laughed. "It was supposedly the fugitive chase. But I've never had to chase some asshole who was in that kind of shape."

"You got that right," Willie said. "Most of those bastards are drunks just like us."

"Hell, yeah," Dark said. "They're too busy stealing people's shit to worry about getting in shape like that *deer* dude. Damn, baby, that white boy can run."

"Yeah, yeah, yeah," Nelson retorted. "Deer may come and deer may go, but the bull never stops around here."

"Isn't that cows?" I asked.

"Cows, deer. Same thing. They've all got four legs and we eat 'em, right?"

"Good point."

"Good thing they didn't have any of those deer running around in Hogan's Alley," Willie said. "My hunter instincts woulda kicked in and we'd have had deer roasting at our next Lunga party."

We'd spent a short afternoon at the old Hogan's Alley range early in our firearms training, and spent another one there during our last two weeks. The term "Hogan's Alley" derived from a comic strip in newspapers in the early 1900s. Apparently, Hogan's Alley was populated by nefarious scoundrels, assorted bottom feeders, and various thugs of 1920 vintage.

The Hogan's Alley complex, simple and plain, was on one forlorn section of the ranges at the academy. Plywood walls with simulated doors and windows were used with cardboard cutouts of both innocent civilians and bad guys in the training exercises. The agent would walk down the sidewalk as cutouts appeared randomly in the windows and doors. Agent trainees would see the cutouts and draw their weapon, immediately trying to identify if they were facing a friend or foe. The objective was to not only identify the correct person to shoot, but to hit the target in a place where it would do the most damage. Or, as our firearms instructors would say, "To neutralize the suspect."

Originated in the 1920s at Camp Perry, Ohio, the Hogan's Alley concept attempted to provide realistic training in 'Shoot, Don't Shoot' situations. Unfortunately, the training was probably more appropriate to the 1930s or '40s than forty years later when we were in the academy. While the training at Hogan's Alley was fun, it wasn't hard to tell it was far outdated from any situation we'd encounter as agents in the field offices we'd be heading off to.

Identifying the bad guys at Hogan's Alley wasn't a difficult task. Many of them were wearing typical gangster clothing from the 1930s: brimmed hats, double-breasted, pinstriped suits, and were carrying either a shotgun with oversized barrels or a Tommy gun. Most were scowling or had a gaping scar on their face. One or two had an innocent citizen in front of them as a hostage or cover, which made the accuracy of the agent's shot all the more difficult and important.

Gary laughed out loud. "Hell, Willie, you and Boots killed more civilians than bad guys anyhow. If they'd given you a moving target out there, you two would've probably shot yourselves or a couple of us."

"Yeah," Slipper added. "Willie woulda done better out there with his bow and arrow or a spear."

Willie and Boots were two of the more notorious members of the 'Rubber Gun' squad in our class. Both had spent hours of remedial time on the range to make the minimum qualification score of seventy.

Looking hurt, but not that badly, Boots displayed his middle finger and pointed it at Gary.

Dark yelled from the end of the table, "Hey, Boots! Watch where you're pointing that thing."

"Don't worry, Dark," Nelson said with a laugh. "The last thing he's gonna hit is what he's pointing at."

Thirty-Nine

Retrospective

We'd spent the better part of our last week at the academy in an alcoholic haze, struggling to get ourselves packed to head off to our first offices across the country. Starting on Monday, every day of the week was a blur. We'd stuffed books, folders, and notes into boxes along with the clothing we could survive without for a few days. The academy had a fully staffed post office with its own zip code, and we sent box after box off in the mail, hoping it would all arrive safely.

Our staff counselor, Sam Batterson, whom we hadn't seen in a month, showed up one morning and asked us to do an evaluation of our academy training. "I want you all to be truthful," he said, "because we use the evaluations to make the training better for future classes."

Foolishly, I was honest, which was a huge mistake as I'd discover within a week of arriving in Los Angeles.

"Mr. Klein, do you think you know more than the FBI about what types of things you should learn in the academy?" asked the so-called First Man in the office, a Supervisory Special Agent and personal assistant to the SAC.

Trying to cut my losses, I groveled, saying that I was only trying to do what Mr. Batterson had implored us to do, never thinking I'd be soundly chewed out for my honesty. A valuable lesson was learned from that meeting.

On Wednesday night we had an informal party at the Officers Club that included most of the usual group. Dinner was supposed to be part of the celebration, but

Willie and Boots decided to drink theirs. Displaying astute medical knowledge, our class physician went for the basic, high cholesterol double cheeseburger with greasy fries. Gary DeCamp ordered a steak "so rare I've gotta stab it with my fork so it won't run off my plate." Dark Clark, ever health-conscious, opted for salmon, green veggies, and a salad. Jim Nelson and I both went for the prime rib with loaded baked potatoes. Nicole Jackson, who usually ate like a sparrow, selected a few appetizers from the mini-buffet.

Boots proposed the first toast, since he was still sober. "To Nurse Mary, the worst instructor we had at the academy, and the one who displayed great sensitivity when P.J.'s back went out. What was it she said P.J.?"

"You better get yo ass back to class boy or they gonna fire you," I said in my finest Nurse Mary imitation.

"Yeah, something like that," Boots said. "I've gotta nominate her for the Florence Nightingale award for compassion."

Willie raised his glass. "To Marvin Johnson and the magic elixir, 'mother's milk, mother's milk.'"

"Here, here." We all raised our glasses.

"And an honorary award for 'The baby was dead, the baby was dead,'" Nicole added. "Mr. Johnson just had to say everything twice to get the point across, didn't he?"

Same reply from the group with raised glasses clinking together.

"To Doc and Boots," Gary toasted. "Our intrepid streakers and boat thieves. What'll we name that award?" He looked around the table.

"Tom, Dick, and Harry?" I proposed to plenty of laughter.

"That'll work," Willie said. "Don't matter. They're two of the craziest bastards I've ever run across, and that includes some of the Injuns on the res."

"All right, all right." Jim Nelson had been quiet and composed up to that point. "We could probably do this all night, but you'll have to admit we had a lot of laughs in the past four months. My personal favorites would have to be those two bozos from the Ident Division who supposedly taught us all about fingerprinting. Was that the most worthless crap we had or what?"

Glasses again went up. "Here, here."

Nicole was quick with her addition to the list. "You know, I personally think our week of first aid was even more worthless than that. How we ever managed to memorize all of that useless crap...well, I don't know. Maybe we should give an award to P.J. for coming up with the way to regurgitate it all back and at least pass that bullshit test."

"Not so fast my friend," Doc retorted. "Some of us obviously didn't learn it all."

"Yeah, but at least that assured you of your medical degree," I said. "What would we all have done without our class physician?"

Dark, who seemed to be enjoying the festivities as much as the rest of us, grew a little more serious for a moment. "Hey guys, on a serious note, we did lose some classmates, and that's too bad, I think. My man Big Bob was a great guy and he'd have made a great agent. I would love to have the opportunity to work with him someday. Just couldn't cut it on the academic side, but he was a beast on the physical stuff."

"No question about it," I said. "I got pretty close with him and I really hope everything works out for him." I looked at everyone around the table. "But aside from Bob, there were a few we lost that had no business being here in the first place. Remember that teacher with the big boobs who smoked like an old steam locomotive and couldn't even come close to running the two miles?"

The food arrived and we all began digging in. Gary spoke next, but he was starting to slur noticeably. "You know, the guy I've really got to hand it to is Chip Taylor. The first day I saw him I thought, 'What the hell is this guy doing here?' He was a porker."

"He must have taken off at least forty pounds," Boots said.

"Yeah," Willie said, definitely sounding like he was under the grip of the grape. "If he lost it, I think me and P.J. found it."

I laughed. "It was all that free food, dude. Just couldn't hold myself back. Those NA guys were always bitchin' about it, but I was eatin' it like it was going away the next day."

"Jensen's been calling me the Pillsbury Doughboy for a month," Willie complained.

"Same here Willie," I replied. "I suppose we shoulda done a little more running and working out. But no. When given the chance to work out or going out drinking with you morons...well, there really wasn't much of a choice was there?"

Dark raised an arm and flexed a muscle. "It's all about genetics baby. Look at the Doc and Boots. None of us put away as much booze as those two, but neither one of those cats put on a pound here."

Nelson laughed. "Not to change the topic, but you know what's funnier than hell?" It really wasn't a question. "The two guys here with the most background and experience are the ones they're sending to the rubber gun squads. I mean, c'mon. P.J.'s going to the applicant squad. And Doc's gonna be working foreign counter intelligence? Gimme a break."

"Why don't the words 'Doc' and 'intelligence' seem to work in the same sentence?" Nicole nodded her head in agreement with herself.

"Isn't that one of them there oxymorons?" Willie asked as Doc flipped the bird to both of them and went back to swilling his booze. He had two more drinks in front of him.

"Probably," Boots retorted. "But putting Doc on a top secret squad is crazy. C'mon. He can't keep a secret about anything. If he finds something out, he's gonna call me. Next thing we know the Rooskies will be tapping his home phone."

Doc slowly raised his finger again.

Dark laughed with the rest of us. "But seriously, doesn't it seem a little ridiculous to take a guy with a ton of law enforcement experience and hundreds of arrests behind him and put him on a squad that does background checks? Where's the planning in that?"

The Applicant Squad in most offices was notoriously staffed by first office agents, discipline cases, and agents who simply couldn't cut it on the street. It's not dangerous or challenging work, and certainly not a job that agents would aspire to spend their career toiling at.

Willie was always quick with a response. "Nicole's gonna be out there chasin' bank robbers and P.J.'s gonna be breaking up them nasty job applicant crime rings."

"Yeah, and the Doc's gonna be out there in a trench coat and a brimmed hat with sunglasses spyin' on terrorists or something," Nelson added.

Doc raised his finger again, looking disconsolate. "Hey, them little KGB critters better look out. The Doc is on the case. I've seen some of them movies. They're gonna see me everywhere they look. They'll wish they never heard of the Doctor."

"Well, you'll do fine, Doc," I said. "And so will I. It's not gonna last forever. They say we'll be on our first squad for six months and then we get transferred to another one. I'm gonna try to get on the Organized Crime Squad, I think. Those couple of classes we had on the Mafia really got my attention. I'd like to get a piece of that action, to tell you the truth. Sounds pretty interesting to me. Going after all of those mob guys. Cool stuff."

Willie took a bite out of one of Nicole's chicken wings. "It's gonna be fun, but I'll tell you the truth about something. I really wish I felt like I was ready to get out there among 'em."

"You ain't the only one, baby," Nicole shot back quickly. "I'm scared shitless."

"I second that motion," Nelson said. "There are some things I thought they were gonna teach us about that just didn't happen."

"Like what?" Gary asked.

"You name it," Nelson replied. Why didn't we have a whole week of interviewing rather than fingerprinting or photography? Look at what we got out of that. Nothing."

"Good point," Dark said. "When you think about the FBI, you think about guys who're gonna get people to cop out to everything. What'd we get? A couple hours of interviewing?"

"Yeah," Willie added. "And then we were interviewing *each other*. It was absolutely ridiculous, and we barely learned about the basic report form for interviews, let alone how to document an interview. I feel like I'm gonna be flyin' solo when I hit the street."

"It was pretty disappointing," I agreed. "And then they give us a completely useless week of first aid, and another week of fingerprinting. Neither of which will do us a damn bit of good. Not to rub it in, but I'll have to say I'm glad I've got about ten years of that behind me."

"Really," Nicole said. "You'll be way ahead of the power curve. Now all of us have to find a way to catch up."

Nelson's words were starting to overlap each other. "Yeah, we didn't get anything on arrest situations, and when we get out there in our field offices, I assume that's something we're gonna need to do."

"Ya think?" I said. "Just because we got that training on the mats doesn't mean a damn thing. Some of these characters are gonna fight for real. Plenty of 'em did with me and I'm glad I've got that experience behind me. I'm guessing a fugitive or a bank robber is gonna be much more apt to fight than some banker who embezzled money."

"Amen." Willie raised his cup for a toast. We all clinked glasses one final time.

Dark finished his drink. "Well, I'm ready to get out of here. How about you guys?"

"Hell, no." Doc looked directly across the table at Boots. "We're gonna go out and do some serious drinking. Who else wants to come?"

Everyone else took a pass, shaking their heads. "I'm good," I said. "It's pretty late and I need to get some sleep, but don't come roarin' back to the room slamming doors and raising hell with your little buddy again." I looked at Doc and Boots, knowing full well that's exactly what would happen.

And I was right.

Forty
Graduation

The accent was clearly Hispanic, but it was difficult to tell if the man was from a foreign country or had grown up in an American barrio.

Our graduation speaker was the Special Agent in Charge of the San Juan office of the FBI. He was tall, at least 6'2", athletic in appearance, with a dark complexion and jet-black hair combed straight back. He wore an expensive-looking dark blue suit with a dark red patterned tie and heavily starched white shirt.

"My first office in the FBI was Pittsburgh, where I worked fugitives and bank robberies. I had a lot of fun. After a year I was transferred to San Francisco where I worked foreign counter intelligence cases and later worked on the white-collar crime squad. I was a field agent and a relief supervisor, and it was a lot of fun, too. After I left San Francisco, I went to Los Angeles as the supervisor of the applicant squad and later the organized crime squad. I had a lot of fun there, too."

Doc kicked me with his foot as he'd done more than a few times during our weeks at the academy. I glanced at him out of the corner of my eye, and he looked back. We both knew exactly what that signal meant, because it meant the same thing every time it happened between the two of us.

"The bureau sent me to headquarters for three years as the section chief of the Violent Crimes Unit, and that was fun, too." Doc whacked my leg with the back of his hand.

It was starting to sound like the bureau was a picnic, without the ants or mosquitoes. Nothing but fun. But something told me that wasn't going to be the case in Los Angeles, which was to be my first office.

It would have been hard to find a less inspiring or inarticulate presenter than the one we'd drawn for our graduation ceremony. Presumably, the SAC had been flown up to Quantico at considerable government expense to deliver what had to be the most boring and embarrassing speech I'd ever heard. I slowly looked over at the Doc, and we both immediately knew what that meant. *Does the rest of the class and the audience realize what an embarrassment this is? And they talk constantly about 'Don't Embarrass the Bureau.'*

Many of the new agents who were graduating that day had family members and friends in the audience. It was truly a momentous occasion to see their sons and daughters become Special Agents of the Federal Bureau of Investigation.

The graduating class was seated in the front two rows of the lavish and well-appointed auditorium of the FBI Academy, which was about a quarter full of graduates, academy staff, families, and other well-wishers. The theater itself was an impressive setting with spacious seating, wood paneled walls, comfortable plush blue seats, dark blue floor to-ceiling drapes flanking the wide stage, and muted, indirect lighting. Behind the podium hung the American flag and the distinctly patterned flag of the FBI. Everything was inspiring and impressive, except our keynote speaker.

"I'd encourage each and every one of you to take advantage of the fine training you've received here at the FBI Academy," our speaker continued. "You're among the best and the brightest this country has to offer, and we expect the very best out of each of you. I'd be proud to work with any of you someday, and I want to offer my congratulations on your graduation. Best of luck to all of you in the coming years." And mercifully, it ended.

He departed from the podium to be replaced by Sam Batterson, who said, "Would the graduating class please rise and approach the stage?"

We filed toward the steps, and our names were called in alphabetical order. When my name was called, I walked toward the newly appointed Assistant Director of the academy and received my credentials.

I was officially a Special Agent of the Federal Bureau of Investigation, and I think it was the proudest moment of my entire life. And perhaps one of the scariest, because I felt I was going to my field office without the slightest idea how to do my new job.

Forty-One

Why Stop the Party Now?

Most of our classmates immediately gravitated to their families and friends as soon as the graduation ceremony ended. I hadn't seen my wife and eight-year old twins for nearly four months, and it seemed like an eternity. I missed them, as I had since the day we began our training in September. I wished they could have been there to share my joy, but the cost of flights from California and other expenses were prohibitive to our budget. By that night, though, I expected to be back in Los Angeles with them.

The Doc, Willie, and I, having no family present, headed for the food line since our bus wasn't due to leave until noon. We knew we could grab a quick lunch and still be at the airport in plenty of time, since we were on the same flight from Washington National to Chicago. Doc would terminate there, Willie would go on to Albuquerque, and my connecting flight was to Los Angeles.

We arrived at the airport just after one o'clock, checked in, and quickly got our seats assigned. Then we headed to the waiting area for our flight. We were the first and only people there.

"So," Doc said to no one in particular. "We've got four hours until our flight leaves. You guys got any bright ideas?"

"Let's find the bar," I replied.

"Hell, no!" Willie shot back. "Damn drinks there'll break us."

"Who's got a better idea?" I asked.

"Well, let's think about this," Willie said. "Today is Friday and Christmas is only a couple of weeks away."

"And…?" I looked questioningly at Willie.

"Yeah," Doc added. "What the hell does that mean?"

"What happens in big offices on Fridays when Christmas is a week or two away?" Willie said.

Doc and I must have looked puzzled.

"Office Christmas parties?" I ventured.

"Tha's right my man." Willie raised a hand to slap five.

"Which means what?" I asked.

"Which means Crystal City is right across the road," Willie said.

Doc looked even more confused.

Willie seemed to have all the answers. "So…let's go get some free booze."

"Whachu talkin' about, Willie?" Doc appeared to be completely befuddled.

"What I'm talking about is crashing one of them Christmas parties. There's a ton of businesses over there and I'll bet most of 'em are having parties."

"We can't do that, you moron," Doc said.

"The hell we can't," Willie retorted. "Just watch us. C'mon, let's go."

We walked across the causeway between the airport and Crystal City, and Willie pointed out one of the tall, glass enclosed buildings to our south. "Let's give that one a try," he said.

"How in the hell do you propose we get in there?" I asked.

"Easy. Just let me do the talking." Doc and I looked at each other, and I raised my hands, palms up. As did the Doc.

"All we gotta do is act and look like we belong there," Willie said. "Check me out…we're all wearin' suits. C'mon, we'll fit right in. Just follow me."

And he was right. A small cluster of well-dressed partygoers with clear plastic cups in their hands had meandered out into the garden area in front of the huge office building. Several small groups were gathered in the entryway, and the flow of the crowd made it obvious where the party was centered.

"Follow me." Willie turned left into the room where the largest crowd seemed to be. We looked at each other and followed. Willie seemed to have something figured out. Once inside the door, he glanced over at the bar.

"Okay, here's the deal," he whispered conspiratorially. "All we've gotta do is hear the bartender's name from someone. He doesn't have a clue who in the hell any of these people are. They just hire 'em to serve drinks. If you look like you belong, you belong."

Momentarily, a reveler walked up to the bar. "Hey Jerry, gimme another beer will ya?" He held up an empty bottle of Guinness Dark as Willie looked back at the two of us, minions following his every move. I shrugged and looked back at the Doc.

Armed with all the information he seemed to need, Willie swiftly stepped up to the bar. "Jerry, I've got some of my clients with me. Can you get us a few drinks? What do you guys want?" Jerry began taking our orders and pouring our chosen libations into cups.

"You are one smooth-talking son of a bitch," Doc said as we glided toward a table.

"Thank you. Thank you very much. Why don't you guys save me a chair? I need to make a run to the little agent's room."

An hour passed, as did more than a few drinks. It seemed like we were right back in our natural habitat. We landed at a table and ordered a few more rounds of drinks. Doc stuck with his old standby of beer. I nursed my standard vodka and tonic. Being the supposedly *responsible* one of the group, I looked at my watch.

"Hey," I said. "Look at the time. We've gotta get back to the airport. Our flight takes off in an hour." I could tell my words weren't distinct, my head was on a merry go-round, and my legs felt like they were each in business for themselves.

Doc looked around. "Where's Willie?"

Willie had never rejoined us.

"Beats me," I replied.

"Have you seen him wandering around in the crowd?" Doc asked.

"I saw him over there." I pointed to a corner of the large conference room. "He was talkin' to some bimbo. I don't have any idea what happened after that. I haven't seen him since, and that was over an hour ago. C'mon Doc," I said. "We've got to get the hell out of here. We're gonna miss the damn plane. Are you ready?"

"We gotta find Willie." Doc was falling all over himself, leaning into me for balance which, given my condition, probably wasn't one of the brightest ideas he'd had all afternoon. But our class physician would readily admit he wasn't usually invited to bring potato salad to the monthly meeting of the Mensa Society, particularly when he was hammered.

"Maybe he went back to the airport," I said. "Let's haul ass or we'll miss our flight." And off we went, dodging rush hour vehicles and taxis rocketing down the causeway, and stumbling through cabs and cars in the parking lot and people in the airport. Luckily, it was pre-9/11 days, so all we had to do was show our credentials and sign a form to avoid the metal detectors.

The waiting area for our flight was empty as we wobbled up to the counter.

"Ready to go." Doc presented his boarding pass and mumbled at the clerk, who had a perplexed look on her face. She quickly looked at me, and I probably didn't look a lot better than he did. Maybe worse.

"Better hurry," she said. "They're about ready to close the doors."

We rumbled down the passageway leading to the plane. A couple of flight attendants greeted us, checked our tickets, and pointed where we would be sitting.

"Ya think Willie is here?" I asked.

"Who the hell knows?" Doc replied. "He's a big boy. I think. I don't have the slightest idea where he might be right now. Been drinkin' too much. Let's find our seats."

No sooner had we found our seats than a female flight attendant came down the aisle. She whispered to me, "The captain wanted me to ask if you gentlemen would like to sit in the first class section?" She was apparently aware we were agents because we'd filled out the "Armed Officers" forms at the gate before we got aboard. And, wearing suits, we probably looked like we belonged in first class.

I looked at her, then over at the Doc. "What do you think? You want to move up to first class?" I spoke as quietly as I could.

"Hell, yes." Doc could barely talk. "Free drinks up there." I held my finger up to my lips to quiet him.

More booze was all we needed, but it also served to make the flight to Chicago go by much more quickly.

After deplaning, we waited at the gate, hoping Willie was onboard somewhere, but we hadn't seen him get on the plane, so it was a mystery to us. Willie never appeared.

Doc and I parted ways and I headed off toward my connecting flight. I wouldn't talk to or see the Doc again until our twentieth class reunion in Las Vegas. Willie was there as well.

"What the hell happened to you?" I asked.

"Too drunk to find the airport. Didja make it to L.A.?" He asked me.

"Yeah. It was a struggle, but I made it fine. So what did you wind up doing?"

"Spent the night at a hotel in Crystal City," he said. "Oh my God. Some things never change."

"Let's get a beer," Willie said.

And so we did.

Epilogue

My first field office after New Agent Training was Los Angeles. I was scared to death when I reported, despite having been a police officer for more than nine years. One thing I *did* learn at the FBI Academy was there was nothing about being an officer or detective with a police department and being an FBI agent that were the same.

But I was sure that, like my own former department, and virtually all other law enforcement agencies in the United States, there would be a field training program of some sort. Surely I would be assigned to work with a more senior agent to "learn the ropes."

I was wrong.

Newly minted "baby agents" were assigned to a squad and they were on their own, unless a senior agent took pity to teach them some of the ropes. I had to ask a lot of questions and I don't know how many times I heard a response like, "Didn't you learn that in the academy?" And, more commonly from my supervisors after being assigned a case I was clueless how to handle, "Look it up in the MIOG." There were a ton of forms I'd never heard of and paperwork that I didn't have any idea how to do. I quickly discovered the best resource I had available was our squad secretary.

She would always take the time to help me figure out how to do my reports. But she couldn't tell me how to go about conducting an investigation. "It should be in the MIOG."

I got tired of hearing that. I felt like Indiana Jones in *Raiders of the Lost Ark*, when he and his partner were chasing Nazis on horseback.

"What are we doing, Indy?" his Arab partner asked.

"I don't know, I'm making this up as I go along," Jones replied.

Rotating to an Organized Crime squad was even worse. My supervisor, a short and skinny blue flamer, would sit in his office puffing on a cigar and assign new cases as they came into the squad. I once asked him what I was supposed to do with a case, and he replied, "That's your job. You figure it out." Which didn't help a lot.

Within months he assigned me to a case involving a wiretap. My job was to get the affidavit from an Assistant United States Attorney in San Diego and get it signed by a federal judge in Los Angeles. That part was easy, but then came the hard part. Once we went up on our phone lines, we had to monitor them twenty-four hours a day. Here I was, a puny GS-10, brand-new agent, and I had to figure out how to schedule that for seven days a week. We had authority to go a full month. I had a dozen senior agents working *for me.* Luckily, two of them took me under their wings for a few days and explained what I needed to do. I had to advise San Diego and eventually Las Vegas of any pertinent calls, and there were plenty of them. If that wasn't enough, I had to list calls and complete a report to the authorizing judge every week. In person. And then we were granted an extension for another month.

Never in my life had I felt so lost and confused. I was putting in fourteen or sixteen hour days just trying to keep my head above water. In fact, there were a couple times when I drove my truck and camper down to the office, parked near the telephone monitoring station, and slept in my camper. Sometimes I didn't see my family for three or four days.

I was lucky enough to get out of Los Angeles after about two years. My family and I couldn't handle the stress, and I was becoming a weekend alcoholic. After volunteering for an undercover assignment in the Midwest, I wound up in a three-man resident agency (RA), a small satellite office more than 250 miles away from our headquarters city. It was like learning the whole shebang all over again, because my senior resident agent thought I should know everything after having been in the bureau for about two years. He was busy and didn't have time for me, so my savior became another senior agent in a nearby RA. He was willing to tell me how to do what I needed to do, and helped me with paperwork. After a year or so, I felt somewhat competent.

As the years went by, I had several opportunities to go back to the academy for in-service training classes. Changes in the physical plant at the academy were becoming more apparent in the late 1980s. A new dorm was built, but the major advance was the construction of a new Hogan's Alley. It was hardly an *alley* anymore, modernized, and never to be confused with the 1930s version we used for training. They had a street scene with various businesses including a drugstore, a bank front, and even a motel. New agents could now benefit from more realistic arrest scenarios than we did by practicing arrest techniques in our dorm rooms.

While those additions were commendable, I talked with many new agents who had just graduated in the late '80s and into the '90s to see if some of the topics we were taught (first aid, fingerprinting, photography with ancient cameras, etc.) were still being covered. It wasn't until I talked to an agent who had graduated in 1997 that I learned at least some of the useless subject matter had been either minimized or eliminated from the program.

In contrast to what was given to us, I discovered the academy had instituted a process of using actors for arrest problems in conjunction with the new Hogan's Alley.

Agents are now being trained in terrorism, and the first aid classes have gone from a week to a few hours. While we had virtually no training in courtroom testifying, new agents now go through Moot Court and get an opportunity to be on the witness stand. Fingerprint classification gets a quick review as opposed to the week we received. New agents learn how to dust for prints and collect them as evidence. Realistic training with 'Shoot, Don't Shoot' videos has been incorporated as a part of the firearms training program.

While the primary emphasis continues to be on defensive tactics, firearms, and legal instruction, new agents are also learning about the collection of evidence and the value of DNA. They no longer have several days of photography with pre-historic cameras, but are trained in the use of digital cameras to record evidence at a crime scene. They receive instruction in the collection and preservation of evidence, and some training is provided using evidence to build a case. They are also put through a couple days of driving training and high-speed pursuits, which is much more valuable than what we received – driving about a mile with our class counselor.

Regrettably, the training they received in conducting interviews and investigations was still lacking. They were being told to consult the MIOG if they had any questions about how to conduct an investigation into the vast array violations the FBI is tasked with investigating. It does not appear, even now, that the FBI has instituted a formal program to mentor new agents once they leave the academy. Frankly, this is unforgivable, and desperately needs to be changed.

In the spirit of fairness, there have unquestionably been some significant changes implemented into the training of new FBI agents. The academy is now twenty weeks long, which is still far less than major agencies such as LAPD, NYPD, and the Los Angeles Sheriff's Department. However, it is clearly an improvement over what agents received twenty years ago. And while that may not appear to be important, consider the fact that those agents who were inadequately trained at the outset of their careers are now running the bureau.

In-service training programs are excellent for those agents who desire to learn a specialty, such as computer crime, foreign counter intelligence, and terrorism.

The old days of 'we're the FBI and we'll train 'em our way' have apparently changed to adapt to modern times, and it is no longer a situation where, as one pundit put it, "FBI agents are trying to find Osama Bin Laden, but are still being trained to arrest Bonnie and Clyde."

I only wish the training we received had been more in line with modern times.

About the Author

Pete Klismet served his country with two tours in Vietnam on submarines. Following military service, he earned a college degree, then worked for the Ventura Police Department in Southern California. During this time he attended graduate school and earned two master's degrees. He was offered and accepted an appointment as a Special Agent of the Federal Bureau of Investigation, and went through the FBI Academy in Quantico, Virginia. His experiences at the FBI Academy form the basis for this book.

In a twenty-year career with the FBI, the author was highly decorated, served with distinction in three field offices, receiving numerous awards and recognition from the FBI. He was named the National Law Enforcement Officer of the Year by a multi-national organization in 1999 for solving a $60 million dollar international fraud case.

Following his retirement, he accepted a position as an Associate Professor and Department Chair of a Criminal Justice program at a college in Colorado, where he and his wife Nancy currently live.